GUIDE

TO

THORPENESS

(Leiston Station, G.E.R.)

The Home of Peter Pan.

Profusely Illustrated, including Map of

"THE CHILDREN'S PARADISE,"

Sixty Acres of Safe and Shallow Water and Ornamental Islands.

BY

W. H. Parkes.

First published in 1912.

2001 edition published by Meare Publications
Maple Lodge, Barleylands, Aldeburgh, Suffolk IP15 5LW.

Printed in England by Leiston Press
Unit 1b Masterlord Industrial Estate, Leiston, Suffolk IP16 4XS.

ISBN No: 0-9540715-0-6

CONTENTS.

	Page
FOREWORD	5
CHAPTER I—The Thorpe of Yesterday	9
CHAPTER II—The Thorpeness of To-day	18
CHAPTER III—The Kursaal	56
CHAPTER IV—The Meare	64
CHAPTER V—The Children's Paradise	72
MAP OF CHILDREN'S PARADISE ... *(facing page 72)*	
CHAPTER VI—Communications with Thorpeness	79
CHAPTER VII—The Economics of Thorpeness	83
LEASE OF BUILDING SITES	86
CHAPTER VIII—"As Ithers see us"	87
CHAPTER IX—Excursions in the Vicinity	98
ADVERTISEMENTS	108

THE CLUB BOAT-HOUSE—EAST VIEW.

FOREWORD.
By the Editor.

THORPENESS has suddenly been called from obscurity into the proud and brilliant company of East Coast holiday resorts. From the first moment of her debut, her success has been instantaneous, continued and complete. The demand for house accommodation throughout her brief history has always been greater than the supply. During last season—a season which happened to be distinctly below the average on the East coast—every bungalow and indeed every house of any importance on the estate was let, frequently to two and sometimes to three families in succession. Before the end of November over 90% of the new bungalows had been taken, furnished or unfurnished, on lease. Several of the further 20 bungalows since erected were applied for and taken before they were completed.

The reason for this remarkable success is perhaps not far to seek. Thorpeness is in many ways unique. She stands beautifully situated, flanked by the purple heather landwards, and seawards by an orange belt of wide sand-banks—the finest sands on the Suffolk coast. She is select, yet unconventional. She is not—nor ever will be—vulgarised by a pier or esplanade or ———— minstrels or "nosebag trippers." Her Fairy Godmother has presented her with rights from the old feudal manor which protect her and her alumni on every side. She is secluded, yet easy of access. A covered motor car meets all G.E.R. trains at Leiston Station by appointment. She will soon have a convenient Station of her own. Her growth is the outcome of a plan carefully thought out in every detail before a single step was taken towards her sure development. She owns a commodious Kursaal, with balconies overlooking the sea on one side and commanding on the other the tennis courts, the bowls and croquet lawn and the flower-borders of the pleasure grounds. The Club possesses every convenience for both sexes, including lounge, reading and ladies' room, circulating library, with an excellent refreshment service and a choice cellar. There are also private bathing cabins for members. The village further possesses a large garage and ample stable accommodation, while the new "Dolphin" hotel is now ready to receive week-end and other visitors.

The deservedly popular Aldeburgh Golf Links are within a quarter-of-an-hour's run of this garden village by the sea. But the peculiar and crowning glory of Thorpeness lies in her Meare, "The Home of Peter Pan"—an artificial lake covering over 60 acres, with tree-planted islands especially furnished with huts, tents and forts as the Children's Playground. This inland sea is as safe as it is fascinating for little folk, its maximum depth being only 2-ft. 6-in. There is a handsome Boat Club-house with loggia, where tea and refreshments are served, overlooking the lake.

The Thorpeness Bungalows are the creation of an artist, MR. FORBES GLENNIE, and are as practical as they are picturesque. Every bungalow is supplied with water of the purest description from a deep well situated far from the Township and away from any possible source of contamination. The rents of all houses on the estate, if taken by the year, cover rates (including the water rate), taxes and all out-going expenses, except the acetylene gas, which is supplied through shilling-in-the-slot or ordinary meters. In short there are no "extras" —those grim familiars of the seaside,—even the upkeep and furnishing of the very gardens being included in one fixed price. If this is taken into consideration, it will be found that the rents at Thorpeness are from 15 to 20% cheaper than those of any other town on the East coast offering similar advantages. And these advantages are many.

For the young and active there is golf (on the adjacent Aldeburgh links); lawn tennis, croquet, and bowls at the Kursaal; sailing or rowing or punting on the lake; fishing in the well-stocked Meare fish preserves; bathing on the sands; kite-flying, clock-golf, stump cricket and rounders on the extensive Playing Fields. For the elders seeking health and renewed vigour to face the work of another year, rest—rest in the East coast air that is as wine to visitors, rest amidst peaceful surroundings and homely comfort "far from the madding crowd." Above all, for the children Thorpeness offers a veritable Paradise in the world of make-believe. Study the monstrous and amazing chart of The Meare, wherein the glamour of STEVENSON and BARRIE takes concrete form. Where else within the four seas shall the boys discover their Pirates' Lair, their Roaring Camp, their Smugglers' Cave, their Brigands' Haunt? Where else shall the girls possess their Peggotty's Hut or their Magic Pavilion, in which to offer the hospitality of Arabian nights under the special protection of the Pari-Banou?

Encouraged by the success of last year's "Guide to Thorpeness" (now out of print) we offer this entirely new edition brought up-to-date and with numerous further illustrations in the hope that it will meet with an equally favourable reception from the public at large.

"I will, if you please, take you to the house and introduce you."

Sir Humphry Davy.

A COTTAGE AT THORPENESS.

CHAPTER I.

THE THORPE OF YESTERDAY.

> "Come unto these yellow sands
> And then take hands:
> Courtsied when you have and kiss'd
> The wild waves whist,
> Foot it featly here and there."
>
> *Shakespeare.*

THE seaside hamlet of Thorpe, now re-named and recognised by the General Post-office as Thorpeness, to distinguish it from the 16 other Thorpes in England, lies about 1½ miles North of the well-known town of Aldeburgh, but, owing to the lack of proper road communication, is at present more conveniently approached by motor from Leiston station on the Aldeburgh branch of the G.E.R.

Little is known about the early history of Thorpe, except that formerly it had a chapel, St. Mary's, which was standing for some time after the Restoration, but is now demolished; only a small portion of the original walls remaining to mark the site of the once famous shrine. For many years, however, the little village has been known to the faithful few as an ideal seaside Summer resort. The County gentry, retired military officers, well-known artists and well-to-do merchants from Norwich, Ipswich, and even London, have built and occupied bungalows on the edge of the rolling sand dunes overlooking the North sea.

The Thorpe of yesterday, the Thorpeness of to-day, is situated at the furthermost Southern extremity of the Manor of Leiston, which appears to be mentioned in Domesday book as "Lehtuna" and then formed part of the vast estates in Suffolk possessed by Robert Mallett, son of William Mallett, who came to England with the Conqueror. "Lehtuna"

THE NESS.

further appears to have been a large Manor comprising other inferior Manors. The Manor was subsequently granted by a charter of Henry II to Randall or Ranulph de Glanville and in or about the year 1182 the latter built and endowed an Abbey and gave to the Abbot and Convent thereof the Manor of Leiston or "Leyston." After the dissolution of the monasteries, the Manor was granted by Henry VIII to Charles, Duke of Suffolk, and the grant included "the wreck of the sea to the said Manor pertaining."

The Duke of Suffolk seems to have held this grant for but a very short period, and then to have given it back to the King in exchange for other lands. The Manor remained in the possession of the Crown until James I granted it to his son Charles, Prince of Wales (afterwards Charles I), but this grant was terminated, and the Manor was then granted by James I to the famous George Villiers, then Marquis, and afterwards Duke, of Buckingham. The grant to the Duke of Buckingham expressly includes the forfeited goods of "Pirates," meaning, no doubt, goods captured from or abandoned by pirates sailing over the foreshore.

Coming to more recent history, the Manor has been in the possession of the Vanneck family since the year 1768, and a document of the year 1796 is in existence by which the first Lord Huntingfield appointed two persons to be Bailiffs of the Manor of Leiston, to seize all wrecks of the sea which should be cast upon the foreshore within the precincts of the Manor.

Apart from their historical value, the above facts possess a present and very practical value for the inhabitants of Thorpeness, inasmuch as the developing Company, SEASIDE BUNGALOWS LTD.—which, for brevity's sake, is usually referred to in this Guide as the Company—have, at a considerable expense, acquired all Manorial rights over their property, and more particularly over the foreshore in front of the said property (*i.e.*, the land lying between the high and low water marks of the sea). These rights entitle the Company to any wreck of the sea that may be cast ashore upon their property. Moreover, the Company, as the owner of this foreshore, can prohibit bathing thereon or therefrom, or persons walking over it during low tide, or persons landing on the foreshore (except in cases of emergency), or putting off in boats therefrom.

It has been, as it always will be, the first object of the Company to preserve the many rare and particular charms and amenities of Thorpeness for the sole benefit of its residents, and the above right will provide an important and powerful weapon of defence against the invasion of trippers and other "undesirables" who too often break in upon the peace and quietude of similar seaside resorts.

This is particularly so, as one of the most attractive features of Thorpeness is the magnificent stretch of sands which already exist, and which seem year by year to increase in width and extent along the whole foreshore of the village, somewhat to the detriment of the fishing community. It may be fairly claimed that there are no other sands of equal extent or beauty on the whole of the Suffolk coast. Not only do these sands afford a delightful playground for the children, but provide peculiarly safe and pleasant bathing, owing to the flatness and softness of the sandy bottom; whereas the general character of the East coast shore is a shingly beach, with a sharp dip immediately behind the wave-line, caused by the scour of the tide, a source of considerable

THORPENESS SANDS.

danger to little children and non-swimmers. Many applications from distinguished visitors in the neighbourhood are constantly being received for permission to erect tents and use the Thorpeness foreshore, but in every case the Directors have felt reluctantly compelled to withhold these privileges from all who were not actual residents of the garden village itself.

Thorpeness is bounded, therefore, on the East by the German Ocean, and a sandy beach inferior to none on the East coast. A few hundred yards to the North, the Ness, a further spit of sand, which is ever increasing in dimensions, runs out into the sea and forms a natural groyne or breakwater, which year by year is apparently throwing the tidal back-eddy, with its destructive scouring action, further South. Careful and continual observations have been taken on the spot, which seem to indicate beyond all doubt that the sea erosion has almost entirely ceased opposite the site of the township, and is making itself felt further South. So satisfied are the Company of this important fact that they insert in all their leases a clause providing for the *ipso facto* determination of such lease in the event of damage by the sea.

Northward, various public footpaths and the high-hedged sandy lanes so frequently met with in Suffolk, lead to Leiston (*vide* Excursions). The public road lies for the most part across wide stretches of heath land, glorious in May when the frequent gorse is aflame with yellow bloom and yet more majestic in August, when clothed in the imperial purple of the heath.

To the West the main road runs almost in a bee line

with arable fields on either side, across the railroad to further heather land and copses of Scotch firs (behind which the Parish Church and The Ogilvie Almshouses stand lost to sight) till it bisects the main road from Leiston to Aldeburgh at the little village of Aldringham.

To the South the sand dunes again stretch away in narrow, uneven ridges until they reach the old mouth, now silted up, of the river Hundred, a few yards to the South-east of the Jubilee Bridge. Beyond this bridge a wide expanse of shingle continues up to the Northern-most houses of the ancient town of Aldeburgh (*vide* Excursions), which stands some mile and a half to the South, silhouetted against the sky line as it follows the curve of the bay Eastward and seaward.

Behind this line of grass-grown hummocks caused by the blown sand of countless years, lies the reflooded Mere, covering an area of over 60 acres to the South and South-west of Thorpeness. This Mere, or as it was spelt in Queen Elizabeth's time, "Meare," in former years and apparently down to the early part of Queen Victoria's reign, covered a much larger area of land, with an outlet to the sea known as "Alnmouth" or Thorpe haven.

There could still be found, not many years ago, amongst the old Thorpe fishermen, those who remembered Thorpe haven being full of Dutch *bumboots* which had taken refuge there under stress of weather. This Thorpe haven, as shown in a map of Queen Elizabeth's time preserved at the British Museum, was considerably to the North of the present extinct haven. The Hundred river at that time flowed into the Meare at the North-west corner thereof. The Meare and the Hundred river were

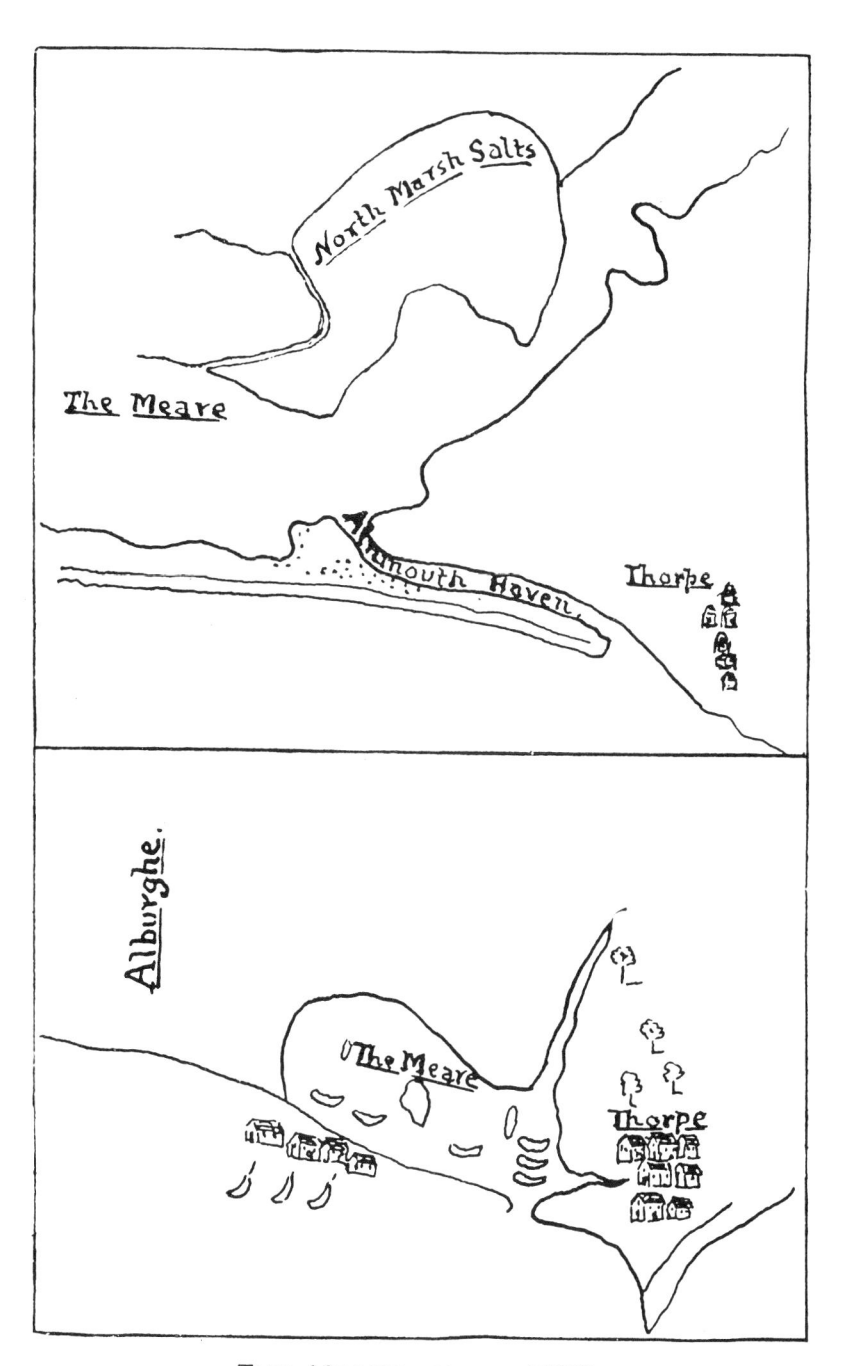

THE MEARE. CIRCA 1588

no doubt at one time tidal, but the outlet, probably owing to the diminution of the back water from the uplands, became silted up and the sea water consequently could no longer enter into the Meare. So long as the sea water flowed into and out of the Meare at every tide, the silt and alluvial deposit brought down in the waters of the Hundred river were carried out to sea, and the Meare was probably fairly deep. When the Meare became non-tidal, this silt was collected in the sometime haven, which thus became shallower and shallower.

In order to ascertain as far as possible the old bounds of the Meare, reference may be made to the foregoing map of Queen Elizabeth's time, from which it would appear that the water extended from Thorpe village to the town of Aldeburgh, and from the Benthills adjoining the sea-shore to a considerable distance inland. Later maps in the British Museum confirm these boundaries. The 1882 Ordnance Survey shows the land covered with water, bounded on the North by the roadway leading from Thorpe village to Aldringham in part, and by lands now forming a portion of the Company's estate in remaining part; on the East by the Benthills, and on the West by the Aldeburgh and Saxmundham branch line of the Great Eastern Railway. Thorpe Meare, so far as it lies within the bounds of the Manor of Leiston, formed part of the commons or waste lands of the Manor granted, as stated above, by King James I to George, Earl of Buckingham, in 1618-1619. The boundary of the Manor on the South followed the boundary line dividing the parishes of Aldeburgh and Aldringham-cum-Thorpe.

A few years ago the Meare was emptied of water, as a result of the drainage of certain marshes in the parish of Aldeburgh, lying to the South of the Meare, and the property of Captain Vernon-Wentworth, R.N., leaving a flat and barren waste where the water previously stood.

It was only in the Autumn of 1912 that the Company, having purchased the site of the old Meare, proceeded at once to prepare, under the direction of the Estate Engineer, for the re-flooding of the entire area by the erection of the necessary embankments, the provision of intakes, outfalls, sluices, and other devices for controlling the head of water, which was obtained by damming the river Hundred at a convenient position.

A full description of the Meare, together with a map and an illustration of the Boat-house, are given in a separate chapter.

CHAPTER II.

THE THORPENESS OF TO-DAY.

"Green Earth has her Sons and her Daughters,
And these have their guerdons; but we
Are the wind's and the sun's and the water's
Elect of the sea."

Algernon Charles Swinburne.

AN idea of the disposition and character of our garden village now in the making is best obtained by starting from the Kursaal and completing a circuit of the Company's township. Perhaps one of the most peculiar features of Thorpeness is that, though the township is still in the initial stages, there are no suggestions of unfinished ends. The Company are evidently determined that their village by the sea shall not suffer from "growing pains." There is no trace of those confused and untidy wastes, with derelict plots for sale and lonely buildings dabbed about at random, which are generally associated with the development of a new building estate. By cunningly availing himself of the lie of the land, the Architect has virtually completed the outer periphery of the village and will now fill in, section by section, the interior of the township. Under this orderly treatment Thorpeness is growing, and will continue to grow as gradually and imperceptibly as the sand dunes at her feet. Even on Lakeside the $11\frac{1}{2}$ acres of uplands lying between the open common and the North margin of the Meare (*vide* p. 36), where building operations are not expected to recommence till next Autumn, the broad Lakeside avenue and its transverse cross roads have been neatly cut out. All the avenue trees and many of the standard trees in the future gardens have already been planted; the wide quay and landing stage which forms the central feature of these shores completed; and the whole of the 40 or more available plots marked out so that prospective lessees can see and select on the spot instead of trusting to a flat and often misleading ground plan. It is this orderly progression and prevision of the township that cannot fail to impress itself upon the most casual observer.

Full advantage has been taken of the conformation of the land, which rises as a semi-circular hill to an altitude of 32 feet above mean sea level. The shape of the building estate may be likened to that of an open fan lying on the sea-shore and radiating North, West and South. It is now—and will still remain when completed to its last brick—a village with no mean street, a medal with no reverse, a well-balanced picture with no back view. The houses in the very centre of the scheme will look upon ornamental open spaces; the houses upon the outer periphery of the township, already completed, all command extensive views of gorse-grown common, lake or sea. The crown and climax of the whole design—the Mermaid hotel, looking over the red and gabled roofs that lie grouped around its feet—will stand "the cynosure of neighbouring eyes" and dominate the surrounding sea and country on every side.

THE KURSAAL, facing Eastward and seaward, is built upon the highest point of the sand dunes and in a central position of the sea frontage, and is flanked by a gaunt old ship's windmill whose business is to pump water for the

Tennis courts, the Croquet ground, Bowling green and the extensive Flower gardens. Beyond these pleasure grounds is a wide open space, which will eventually be bisected by a spacious tree-planted avenue, leading in a semi-circular sweep to a Public Place faced on the West by one of the main architectural features of the new Town, The Rows. These Rows, which will probably be built next year, will comprise a series of shops under a covered arcade, suggested by the well-known Rows in Chester city. The roof of the arcade will be approached both by wide public stairs and inclined ways—for perambulators, etc.—and not only form a convenient promenade, but also give access to the series of important residential flats which are to be erected above the shops. The height of the shops, with their basement accommodation, has been designed at such a level that the lower or sitting rooms of each flat will look over the pleasure grounds of the Kursaal, the rising sand dunes to the East and the roofs of the houses below them on the West, thus commanding uninterrupted views of the sea, the Meare and the surrounding landscape on every side. These flats will possess all the accommodation of the standard Thorpeness bungalows. The two ends and centre of this imposing block of buildings, which will be treated in the black-and-white school, will be balanced by "Gates." We will now leave the Kursaal by its main East entrance and turning to the right, we immediately come upon some of the most important of all the various groups of bungalows.

THE BENTHILL BUNGALOWS are only six in number, and it is a noteworthy fact, as evidence of their popularity,

THE BENTHILL BUNGALOWS.

BUNGALOW INTERIOR.

that they are all taken upon lease. Situated as they are upon the sand dunes, commanding an unbroken view of the Thorpeness sands and North sea to the East, they are bounded to the West by that part of the Kursaal pleasure grounds known as "The Wilderness," which is already laid out with pines, gorse, broom, tamarisk and other appropriate sea plants. The peculiar charm of the surrounding Benthills has been carefully preserved in the wild garden plots which front each of these bungalows. They are dotted with great tussocks of Bent grass, arranged in most admired disorder and interspersed with clumps of gorse and broom, flanked on all sides by a tamarisk hedge. Each of these houses is provided with a well-designed loggia overlooking the sea, large enough to permit of breakfast or luncheon being taken therein during the hot Summer weather. The interior of these bungalows, which have had to be specially designed to meet the peculiar shape of the dunes on which they are built, comprises a large sitting-room, five bedrooms, a kitchen and the usual offices. By kind permission of a lady resident, we are enabled to give a photograph of a corner of one of these sitting rooms. The site of some old stabling and one of the old Thorpe bungalows—now removed to North End—has been railed off and provided with a terrace and seats for the private use of members of the Kursaal. Continuing our way Southward, we pass some old cottages which formed part of the original fishing village of Thorpe and arrive at

THE DUNES BUNGALOWS. There are four of these houses, No. 1 a detached building facing East, and the other three placed in a row at right-angles to No. 1, facing the South. They are built of the fireproof material known as "H.P. Asbestos slabs," supplied by Machin & Koenig, of London and elsewhere, and with their heavy gable ends and balconies overlooking the sea, form an imposing architectural feature of the new Township.

The internal accommodation of these buildings is both extensive and convenient, comprising, besides a large living room, kitchen and the usual offices, including two E.C.'s (one on the first floor) no less than seven bedrooms. These Bungalows are in great demand both because of their splendid sea views, their numerous bedrooms and their central position. Turning the corner, we find ourselves near another of those open spaces which are such a marked feature in the planning and laying out of Thorpeness, namely—

THE VILLAGE GREEN, an extensive stretch of neatly-kept grass lawns between wide main roads and gravel cross paths. The lawn on the North side of the Green is protected by old-fashioned posts and chains, having in its centre a shallow round pond with a gravel path running round it and a decorative cluster of feathered reeds in its centre. Marshalled round the Green are some of the chief public buildings of the Garden village—the Estate office; the important arched Gateway, with a brick stile on either side, leading to the Pavilion, the Playing Fields, and The Netherlands; the Motor Park and shelter; the Boat Clubhouse, with its ornamental clock tower and porch over the front door; and the South entrance to Barrie's Walk.

THE ESTATE OFFICE, clearly indicated by its prominent wrought-iron Tabard sign, is a particularly pretty little

THE VILLAGE GREEN, THORPENESS.

building in black-and-white, with a gently persuasive air about its exterior as who should say, "We are here to please and satisfy." It is worth while entering the commodious office, if only to study the large map of the Township, which, with coloured drawings and photographs of Mr. Forbes Glennie's work, is exhibited upon its walls. To the South, under the arched gateway are seen The Netherlands and The Playing Fields, situated on some five acres of meadow land reclaimed from the Meare.

THE NETHERLANDS. As will be seen by the accompanying map, these meadows, which are virtually bounded by the Meare on three sides, have been drained and divided to the East by two wide dykes—the East dyke and the West dyke—which form a raised causeway giving access to the 14 building plots (exclusive of the Estate office) called, because of their situation, The Netherlands. These plots are divided by a series of transverse ditches, which are connected in various places by culverts under the road, with the West dyke, thus preventing stagnation and securing a free circulation of the surrounding waters. Both the main dykes have direct communication, through trapped "trunks," with the Meare and are also provided with an outfall into the river Hundred below the main dam. Consequently this entire water area can be emptied and refilled at will, the whole operation taking only a few hours.

A perfectly delightful bungalow—The Tulip Cot—has been erected on plot 1, next to the Estate office, as an example of the fanciful Dutch feeling which will be preserved in the external elevations of each of these Netherlands houses. One peculiarity of these buildings

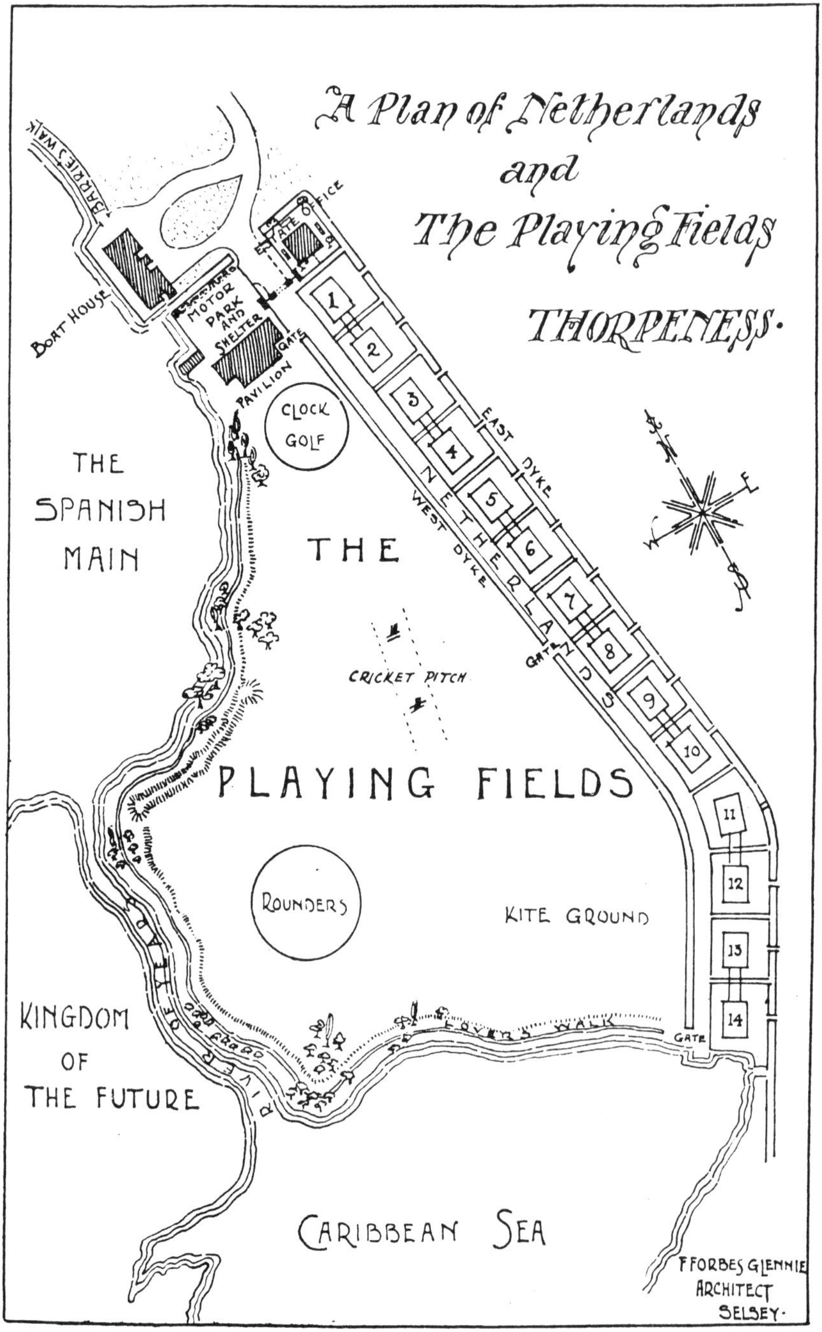
A Plan of Netherlands and The Playing Fields
THORPENESS.
BARRIE'S WALK
BOAT HOUSE
GATE OFFICE
MOTOR PARK AND SHELTER
GATE
PAVILION
CLOCK GOLF
THE SPANISH MAIN
THE
PLAYING FIELDS
EAST DYKE
WEST DYKE
NETHERLANDS
GATE
CRICKET PITCH
ROUNDERS
KITE GROUND
KINGDOM OF THE FUTURE
RIVER STYX
LOVERS WALK
GATE
CARIBBEAN SEA
N
E
W
S
F FORBES GLENNIE ARCHITECT SELSEY.

is that they have two fronts, one facing the Causeway and the Meare and the other the intervening sand dunes and the sea. The problem of how to hide what an Irishman calls "The Glory-hole" or back yard from the general eye has been solved by extending a trellis screen from the South wall of one house across the dividing ditch to the North wall of the next building, the back entrance and offices to each pair of houses facing alternately South and North.

The accompanying pen and ink sketch of the Tulip Cot conveys some idea of the quaint and fascinating form of the house, but naturally misses the coquetry of colour —the vivid green of the shutters; the white of the walls; the yellow and red stripes of the Tulips, recalling the

NO. 1. THE NETHERLANDS.

floral emblems on the stern of a Dutch barge; and the red tone of the Mansard roof—which distinguishes this echo of Amsterdam from any other building in Thorpeness. The internal accommodation consists of: on the ground floor a large living room, 22-ft. by 13-ft. with windows looking East and West, a good dining room 16-ft. by 10-ft.; kitchen, offices and two E.C.'s; on the first floor besides two smaller bedrooms, one large ditto, 18-ft. by 11-ft., giving on to a covered verandah overlooking the full expanse of the Westering Meare; on the second floor two bedrooms leading on to another covered verandah which commands the entire seascape from Sole to Aldeburgh Bay. A little footbridge spans the East dyke and leads straight on to the sand dunes and the beach, while opposite the very front door lie

THE PLAYING FIELDS. The convenient little Pavilion stands immediately on the right upon entering the fields and facing South, overlooks the Clock Golf ground, which was laid out to the special design and under the superintendence of Capt. C. S. Wood, the popular Secretary of the Aldeburgh Golf Club. Some yards further on is the raised and levelled pitch devoted to Stump Cricket and practice at the nets, which will doubtless later on develop into a complete Cricket ground, while still further South another circular lawn of level grass, some 35 yards in diameter, is set out with the usual stakes and stumps for the fine old English village game of Rounders. Ample room is left elsewhere for Kite flying and other pastimes. In short the whole of this wide and sunny close has been devoted specially for the Children who are too young to participate in the more advanced games at the Kursaal, and it is believed that this large private and select recreation ground will be almost as popular as the Meare itself amongst the many out-door attractions Thorpeness offers her favoured little folk. A very small subscription entitles families or individuals to the use of these Playing fields and Pavilion, which are available at any time during the day. The subscription will cover the use of all necessary equipments, such as Rounders stumps and bat, Cricket net and stumps, but not bats or balls for Cricket or balls for Rounders or Golf accessories.

All round the margin of this portion of the Meare—from "Caribbean Sea" to "Spanish Main"—there runs a serpentine tree-planted pathway, Lovers' Walk, slightly raised above the meadow level from which the players at their various games can be conveniently observed, if the strollers be not too much engrossed in "each other's own best company."

THE MOTOR PARK AND SHELTER. Immediately opposite the Estate office is the entrance to the Motor park, a spacious gravelled yard leading to various shelters capable of temporarily accommodating the cars of the large number of visitors who daily bring parties for boating on the Meare throughout the Summer season. Bicycle stands are also available. The Caretaker's cottage is placed in the steep and many-angled roof of this building, which is prolonged Southward to form the above-mentioned Pavilion overlooking the Playing fields.

THE BOAT CLUBHOUSE. This handsome building is fully described in Chapter IV dealing with the Meare.

BARRIE'S WALK. Immediately to the North of the Boathouse landing stage stands one of the three gates giving admittance to this broad walk, (named, by permission, after the immortal creator of Peter Pan) which runs in a semi-circle over 220 yards long round the entire Haven bay and projecting some 50 yards into the Meare, finishes at a slightly raised jetty with a weather-beaten and ancient marine capstan as its terminal. The whole of this broad walk is separated from the surrounding public paths and roads by a light trellis-work fencing, the posts and rails being in red, while the trellis panels and cappings are painted white. The second and main entrance gate is placed in the middle of this semi-circle and opens upon the main road. The third of these gates is symmetrically placed mid-way between the main gate and the jetty terminal and leads on to the Lakeside road. A small landing stage projects into the lake opposite both of these last-mentioned entrances. Between the trellis screen and the Walk are raised flower borders with a backing of ornamental trees and Bamboos and a front border of grass. At the water's edge, running round the entire semi-circle, stands a line of Silver Lombardy Poplars which flutter in everchanging hues of silver and green at the slightest breath of wind. At the back of the Walk garden seats are set for those who wish to lounge away an hour in this sunny and sheltered pleasaunce of Thorpeness.

Continuing our way past The Dunes, we arrive at the first of the Company's bungalows overlooking the Meare, "Alnmouth." In external appearance "Alnmouth" is frankly a specimen of what we may call the "Early Victorian" or pre-Glennie period of Thorpe architecture. Within, however, it is a well-arranged and convenient bungalow of one floor, containing, beside the wide verandah facing South, one sitting room, four bedrooms, kitchen, pantry, wash-house and E.C. with the Company's gas and water laid on. Immediately beyond Alnmouth facing the Arched Entrance to the Playing Fields space has been reserved for the "South gate," the commencement of the new road already alluded to, which will eventually lead to the Rows. We then come to another very favourite group of bungalows known as

THE FIRST BUNGALOWS.

THE HAVEN BUNGALOWS. This series of 12 Bungalows, facing South, commands a splendid and uninterrupted view of the Meare and Boathouse and Barrie's Walk, with its flower gardens, its quays and its semi-circular row of Silver Poplars at the water's edge. The average accommodation of these Haven bungalows is five bedrooms, with two sitting rooms and small kitchen, but some are built more on the lines of the Benthill bungalows and contain, beside one large sitting room (so constructed that it can be converted into two rooms, if desired) six bedrooms, kitchen, two E.C.'s and the usual offices. But no two buildings are exactly alike, either in elevation or

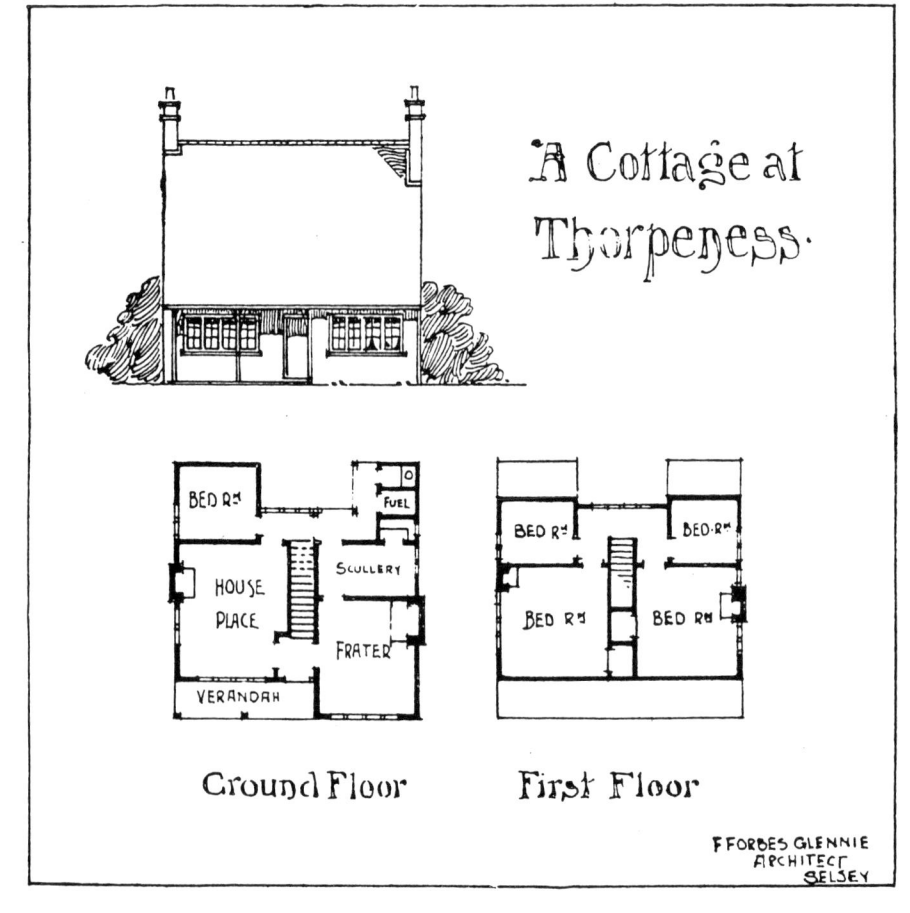

A Cottage at Thorpeness.

Ground Floor   First Floor

F FORBES GLENNIE
ARCHITECT
SELSEY

internal arrangement. Considerable pains have evidently been taken over the colour scheme of these Haven bungalows, which—viewed from the lake—present a frontage as gay and polychromatic as the houses in an Italian street. A really remarkable effect has been obtained by the free use of pink, yellow, white and other colour washes, some of which under the influence of the atmosphere, take on varied and beautiful tones ranging from red rust to a rich purple chocolate. These colours have been applied in combination with the well-known stop-rot "Solignum," supplied by Messrs. Major & Co., of Hull, which has also been used on the external and internal woodwork of a large number of the public and private buildings at Thorpeness. The houses stand, conveniently situated, high above the Aldringham road, which runs between them and the lake.

INTERIOR OF A HAVEN BUNGALOW.

Besides a comfortable porch, large enough to take deck or lounge chairs, each villa has its own little garden, with Lilliputian lawns and miniature borders gay with herbaceous and annual flowers; and planted with sycamore, ilex, ash, oak, or fir trees, while roses, honeysuckle, "Dutchman's pipe," Cotoneaster, vines and other climbers already begin to make a brave show upon every house front. The Company are evidently determined that their new garden village by the sea shall not suffer from the reproach of so many seaside towns or be described, as the poet Keats once scornfully dismissed Margate, as "this treeless affair." As a matter of fact, more than 25 thousand trees, sets, flowering shrubs and creepers, varying in height from 5 to 15 feet, have been planted throughout the Company's estate during the last two seasons. All the "Forest" trees and shrubs have been supplied from the extensive Nurseries of Mr. R. C. Notcutt, of Woodbridge, who has made a speciality of coast planting. At the Western end of these Haven bungalows the road bifurcates and branches left and right round a triangular plot of grass. The left road, skirting the trellised boundary of Barrie's Walk and its West entrance, leads to

BAY BUNGALOWS. Four out of these five houses are built in pairs, standing upon a rising knoll, with ample lawns and gardens stretching to the South and, like the neighbouring Haven bungalows, command the entire panorama of the lake, while from the upper windows the full extent of Aldeburgh bay is seen across the distant sand dunes. The fifth—No. 1—a detached bungalow, has yet to be built. It is evident that the importance of these five buildings in their relation to the general grouping and design of the Haven bay as a whole, has been fully realised and that care has been taken to create an effect worthy of this commanding site. The plot for No. 1 is still vacant, but Nos. 2 and 3 have been treated boldly in the black-and-white school with a black-tiled roof, in marked contrast to Nos. 4 and 5, which are built of wood, and strike an original and pleasing note with their heavy red roofs broken by dormer windows and their projecting upper floor coloured deep black over the pure white of the lower parts of these buildings. The accommodation in all these houses comprises a large living room facing full South and six bedrooms and kitchen, with the usual offices. The tenants of these houses have the further privilege of using the private enclosure lying between the South side of the road and the lake's edge. This enclosure, with its fringe of Lombardy Poplars, is laid out in lawns and flower beds, with comfortable garden seats, from which the life and traffic of the Club boat-house across the water can be watched o' Summer days. Immediately beyond the last of the Bay bungalows commences that portion of the estate which is designed to be figuratively as well as literally "The West End" of Thorpeness, viz.,

LAKESIDE. In response to many enquiries received last year both for building sites and for residences of a somewhat more expensive and luxurious type than that followed in the less grandiose holiday houses which have been already erected and so quickly taken up, the Company have laid out the whole of their land lying North of the Meare and South of the Aldringham-cum-Thorpe Commons in building plots, some of which will be reserved by the Company and others immediately offered on building leases (*vide* p. 86) to persons desiring to erect their own houses on these sunny slopes. The accompanying plan indicates the way in which the Company have treated these eleven and a half acres of undulating arable land which rise steadily to the North-west, so that the houses in the rear will obtain almost as uninterrupted a view of lake and sea as those situated on the water's

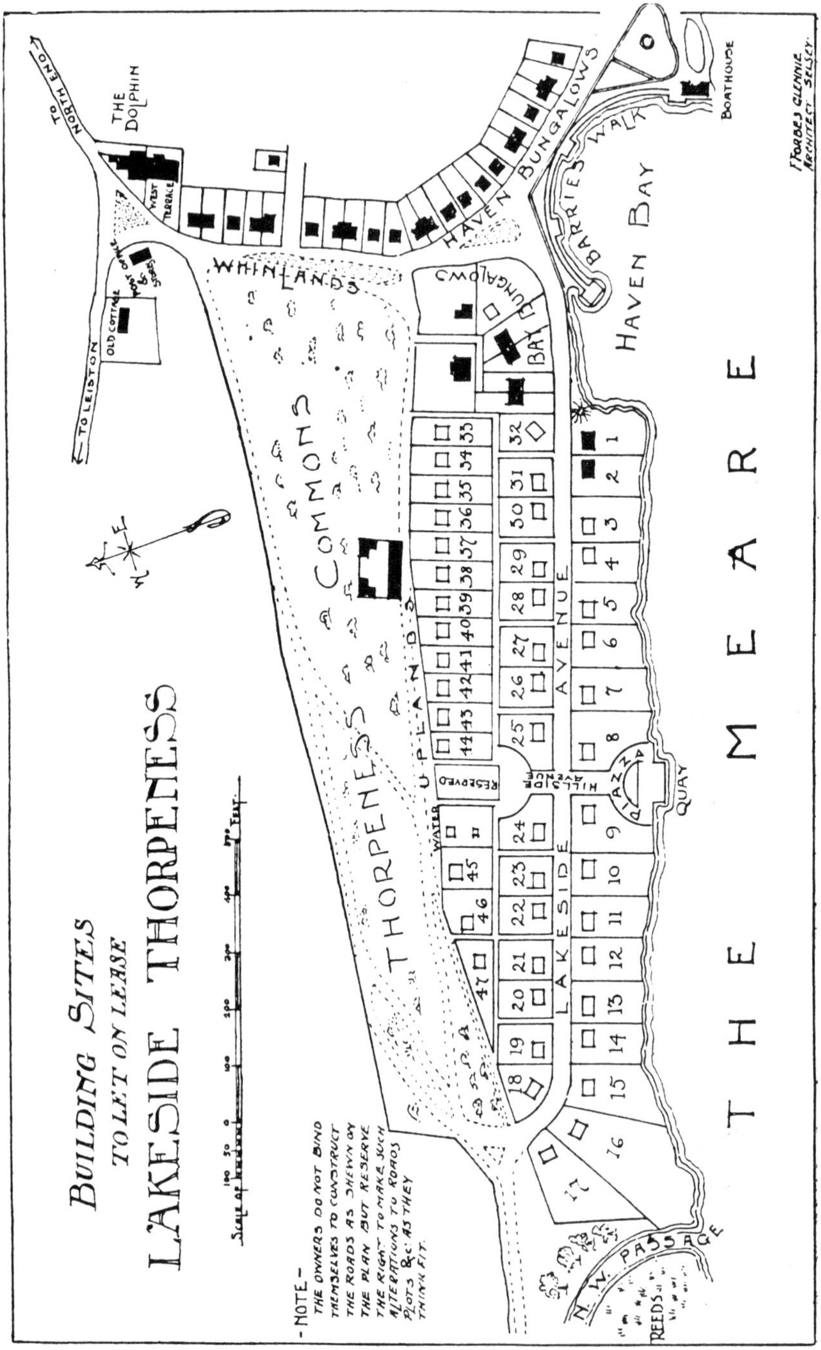

BUILDING SITES
TO LET ON LEASE
LAKESIDE THORPENESS
SCALE OF FEET
- NOTE - THE OWNERS DO NOT BIND THEMSELVES TO CONSTRUCT THE ROADS AS SHEWN ON THE PLAN BUT RESERVE THE RIGHT TO MAKE SUCH ALTERATIONS TO ROADS PLOTS &c AS THEY THINK FIT.
TO NORTH END
THE DOLPHIN
TO LEISTON
OLD COTTAGE
POST OFFICE & STORES
WEST TERRACE
WHINLANDS
HAVEN BUNGALOWS
BAY BUNGALOWS
BARRIES WALK
HAVEN BAY
BOATHOUSE
F FORBES GLENNIE ARCHITECT SELSEY
THORPENESS COMMONS
UPLANDS
WATER
RESERVED
LAKESIDE AVENUE
HILLSIDE AVENUE
PIAZZA
QUAY
THE MEARE
N. W. PASSAGE
REEDS

edge. It will be seen that Lakeside is divided into four parts by two important avenues, one, "Lakeside," running from East to West till it joins the existing public track leading to the Sheepwash level-crossing of the G.E.R.; the other, "Hillside," running from the above-mentioned commons Southward down to the Meare, where it terminates in a wide semi-circular sweep—tentatively named The Piazza—and an important quay and landing stage. It is proposed to place a basin, fed by the overflow from the waterworks, with suitable statuary in the middle of the Piazza. Both these broad roads have already been planted with Lombardy Poplars (set just inside the boundary fences of the building plots) which it is hoped will give character and dignity to the avenues without impeding or breaking the magnificent Southward view from any point. Directly opposite the Piazza quay, on the other side of the Meare, a wide straight channel, called The Sunway, because it runs due South, has been cut through the intervening islands into the Blue lagoon and the line of the Hillside avenue Poplars continued on either bank of the new channel. Viewed from the top of Hillside, the effect thus produced of continuity of roadway and waterway into the very heart of the Meare is peculiarly effective. The Northernmost and highest portion of the land, which may be called "The Uplands," is divided by another occupation road and laid out in a second series of somewhat smaller plots.

The centre plot, looking down Hillside has been temporarily reserved for the future Golf house. Plots have also been reserved round the existing Waterworks for the auxiliary Acetylene gas plant which will in due course supply this portion of the estate.

Lakeside might equally appropriately have been named Henley-upon-sea or after any other famous riverside resort in the Thames valley, for the houses occupying the lower plots will possess all the grace and fascination of riparian villas on the Thames, combined with the champagne atmospheres and exhilarating sea views of the East Coast. Even to-day the prospect from the front windows on Lakeside—which all face due South— is one of singular beauty, commanding as it does the whole sweep of the silver Meare, with its magic archipelago of islands, star-scattered in the circumambient blue below. Beyond the Meare, across the intervening lowlands, rise the tree-crowned heights of Aldeburgh, while away to the South-east, beyond the sand dunes, one catches the glint and movement of the open sea. It is not too much to prophesy that in a very few years' time, when the thousands of Willows, Sallows, Poplars, Elms, Ashes, Sycamores, Horse Chestnuts, Osiers, Atriplex, Tamarisk and other trees have developed, the Meare, as viewed from Lakeside, will present a panorama which, in its infinite variety of form and colour, will be unsurpassed by any beauty spot on English shores.

Each of the sites running down to the waterside will be provided with (or the lessees be permitted to erect) a private landing stage in the Meare and it is proposed, where a tenant desires it, to erect a private boat-house— built in the same style as the particular house to which it belongs—so arranged that the hired or private boat can be floated straight into its shelter from the Lake. In one design we have been permitted to see, an ideal tea-room has been devised over one of these private boat-houses, with double French windows giving upon a balcony which overhangs the lake.

The Company have already built two houses on Lakeside, which may be taken as typical of the class of building to be erected on this section of the estate. No. 1 Lakeside stands in a commanding position at the extreme South-east corner of the Lake and is built of Asbestone, wood and brick. It is approached from the Avenue to the North through a paved entrance to the hall, with the kitchen on the right and a wide staircase leading to the upper floor on the left. Beyond the hall is the house-place or large living room, with its big bay and window seats overlooking the Lake. French windows lead from this room on to the verandah, from which a

NOS. 1 AND 2 LAKESIDE.

broad walk leads across the lawns and their surrounding flower beds down to the private landing stage at the lake's edge. The dining room also leads off from the houseplace and has access to the kitchen, servants' offices and two E.C.'s at the back. There is another room on the ground floor which can be conveniently used as a study or smoking room, or the seventh bedroom. On the upper floor are six bedrooms, bath room with hot and cold water, and W.C. The Company's Acetylene gas, also water supply, are laid on throughout the house.

No. 2 Lakeside is another commodious and attractive thatched house built upon very similar lines and with similar conveniences, but with only five instead of seven bedrooms. Great care has been taken in dealing with the sanitation of these houses, which is effected by cesspool drainage duly trapped and ventilated, the cesspools being constructed of the impervious patent stone rings supplied by the Excelsior Patent Stone Co. of Finedon Sidings, Northants. It has been found that the use of these rings (the lowest one of which is supplied with a solid bottom) is a sure and economical way of cheaply sinking an absolutely water-tight and durable cistern in close proximity to the lake and considerably below the water level thereof.

The usual difficulty encountered in all cesspool drainage to houses where a considerable amount of cooking takes place and bath rooms are in use, is that the large volume of scullery and bath waste water very speedily fills up the largest cesspool and necessitates frequent and inconvenient emptyings. Prevising this objection to cesspool drainage, the Company have provided a large waterproof dead well built with the above rings, which will be used for the W.C.'s alone, while the waste from the scullery sink and from the bath room upstairs are led into a separate receptacle from which they pass through a series of coke breeze filters which arrest all grease and deleterious matter, into a drain leading into the Meare. By this system it is calculated that the dead well, even if the house is occupied to its maximum extent all the year round, will not require to be emptied more than once in every two years at the outside. Following the other road at the Western end of the Haven bungalows, which turns to the right and Northward, we come to

THE WHINLAND BUNGALOWS, being ten houses facing Westward and overlooking the gorse-grown commons, the character of which will be religiously preserved as an open space for all time. These Whinland bungalows, though varying in external form and elevation, in their internal accommodation closely follow those arrangements in the Haven bungalows which have already proved so popular. Like the Haven bungalows, each of these houses is provided with its own little tree-planted front garden, lawns and flower beds. No. 1 and No. 2, Whinlands are detached houses, each having, besides a kitchen and the usual offices, a living room, a dining room and five bedrooms; No. 1 being built of brick, wood and Asbestos Slabs; No. 2 of wood. Nos. 3 and 4, a semi-detached pair, built in a bold design of black and white, have each of them, besides the kitchen and usual offices, six bedrooms and a large living room, which can be divided into two rooms if so desired. No. 5 again is a detached house with the front of its roof broken by a fine dormer gable; it has one large living room (instead of two sitting rooms) and five bedrooms.

Between Nos. 5 and 6 space has been left for the West Gate road, which will eventually lead under an archway in the Rows to the Public Place. Approached by this road and standing well behind the Whinlands group of bungalows is the Generating house which supplies every one of the Company's buildings within the Township with Acetylene gas. Nos. 6 and 7, the Whinlands, are again a semi-detached pair of houses, built in black and white and are perhaps, as regards external elevation, the most striking of this particularly pleasing group of houses. Both these bungalows contain, besides large living rooms, six bedrooms. No. 8 is another detached bungalow in black and white offering the same accommodation as No. 5; while Nos. 9 and 10 form a pair of semi-detached houses each with six bedrooms and a large sitting room.

It is significant of the careful way in which these houses have been set out, that not only do all of them obtain a full view of the open common which stretches for more than a mile to their West, but it is probable that a view of the sea will be obtainable from some of the back windows in every one of these houses, even after The Rows have been built in the centre of the Township. It is not too much to say that a sense of the sea pervades Thorpeness and is preserved in the most inland building on the estate. Beyond the Whinlands is

WEST TERRACE, another relic of the Thorpe of Yesterday, being a series of old fishermen's cottages, which, re-constructed and embellished with pert little porches, stand back from the main road, having grass lawns and flower borders in front of them, and another line of new trees, which in a few years should form a pleasant screen of foliage. Adjoining the West terrace stands the new

DOLPHIN HOTEL on the site once occupied by the old Crown Inn, recently acquired by the Company. The house having been entirely reconstructed and virtually re-built (with further bedrooms and two bath rooms added, the Company's gas and water laid on and a perfect system of Sanitation installed,) was opened in the Spring of 1914 under entirely new management. Messrs. Adnams & Co., the well-known Hotel Proprietors and Brewers,

THE DOLPHIN HOTEL.

of Southwold, have taken over control of this hostelry. As the Hotel is situated within two minutes' walk of the Lake on one side and the sea on the other, commands magnificent views across the open country to the North and West, and offers excellent accommodation on moderate terms it should prove very popular with visitors who do not care to be troubled with the cares of housekeeping. A special feature will be made of catering for week-end or day visitors who come to Thorpeness or the Meare. Opposite the Dolphin, at the corner where the main road branches towards Aldringham, are the temporary buildings used by the

THORPENESS STORES, pending the completion of The Rows. This Establishment supplies goods of every description and the best quality at lowest London prices.

THE POST OFFICE is also temporarily situated in this building. Further Westwards, surrounded by its gay little garden, stands "The Old Cottage," another remnant of ancient Thorpe and a joy to every Artist who visits Thorpeness. It almost seems an anachronism to have introduced Acetylene gas and pure water into this fascinating specimen of other days!

To the right the road trends once more to the sea and, following this road Eastward, we pass the entrance to the large and commodious garage, with its stabling and yard accommodation in the rear. The Company felt compelled to erect these buildings at an earlier date than they had originally intended, owing to the increasing popularity of Thorpeness, which in 1912 attracted a very large number of visitors in motor cars and carriages.

These vehicles caused considerable inconvenience and annoyance to the residents by being left standing in the various open places and public approaches to the sea,

THE GARAGE, THORPENESS.

owing to the fact that there was no proper accommodation available for them. Moreover, several residents brought their own motors and motor bicycles, which they had to house in open and unsuitable cart sheds. To suit the convenience of residents and visitors, the garage provides no less than six "lock up" compartments, while a fireproof petrol store has been built at a safe and suitable distance from the garage and stabling. Petrol, both Pratt's and Shell, and carbide are stocked. Housing accommodation is provided over the garage for the caretaker and his wife, who are thus in continual attendance.

Leaving the grand old barn—our illustration of which is a reproduction, by permission, of a fine oil painting by Edward King now hanging at Sizewell Hall—and the other buildings and cottages pertaining to the Beach farm

THE OLD BARN.

on our left, we arrive at The Old Home. This building, once the property of the Ogilvie Charity Trustees, has been acquired by the Company and converted into six convenient and well arranged houses, which have been greatly sought after since their conversion, both because of their restful outlook upon the dunes and cliffs and their close proximity to the sea and sands. To the East of The Old Home, in quite a considerable compound of its own, overlooking the sea but with its garden (also freshly tree planted) lying warm and protected under the lee of the sand dunes on which this bungalow is built, stands The New Croft, with its front gateway actually giving on to the shelving cliff that leads down to the sands below. North of the New Croft we arrive at the Ultima Thule of the Company's possessions, appropriately called

THE OLD HOME.

THE NEW CROFT.

NORTH END, a triangular piece of cliff and sand dunes where two of the old Thorpeness bungalows which were attacked by the sea in their old positions have been re-erected. There are only three more building sites to be let on lease on this portion of the estate. A few more plots have been reserved by the Company on the very edge of the cliff, where they propose to erect their

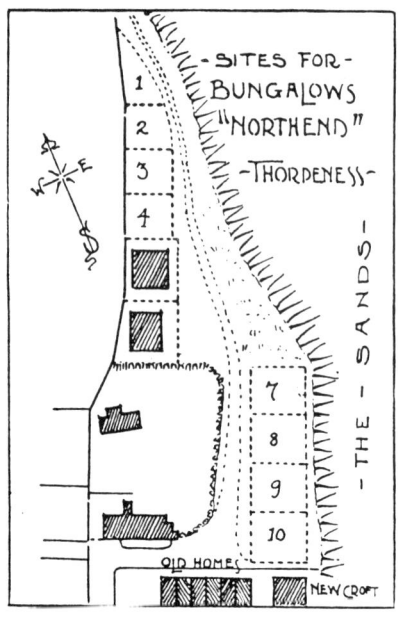

BEACH BUNGALOWS. The Company are not offering these building plots on lease, because they are situated on the only position on the sea front that is at all threatened by sea erosion. The Company propose later on building specially-designed bungalows upon brick piers or piles capable of being removed in the event of the sea overcoming the faggot protection set where necessary at the foot of the cliff.

These Bungalows will be appropriately known as THE BEACH BUNGALOWS. By the courtesy of the Architect we are able to give an illustration of the class of buildings to be used on these sites. It is an interesting fact that these bungalows will be built entirely in sections, so that in case of dire necessity the whole building can be taken to pieces and erected on another site. The internal

BEACH BUNGALOW.

accommodation will comprise, besides a well-designed kitchen with the usual offices, six bedrooms and a large living room 31-ft. long by 11-ft. wide running the entire length of the Eastern or seaward front and provided with so liberal an allowance of windows that, when open, the effect is almost that of sitting out of doors. The living room is connected by a small porch to a balcony, which also runs the full width of the house and leads by easy steps down the shelving sand dune to the beach itself.

Standing as it will upon the crest of the dune, with its bold dormer windows breaking out from the green roof and the white walls relieved by the daring red of the sashes and balustrades, these bungalows should form one of the prettiest of the many pretty groups at Thorpeness.

Retracing our steps, we ascend the sandy lane running Southward towards the Kursaal and pass upon our left, on the crest of the hill, the site which the Company have allotted for the Church of future years, to be called St. Mary's, the name of the old Chapel which once existed and part of the old walls of which may still be traced worked into the outbuildings of the Beach farm. The Company are prepared, when the Township has arrived at a sufficient stage of development, to present this commanding site free of all cost for the erection of the Church, and the Lord of the Manor has undertaken to provide the Eastern window, which has already been designed under his instructions by Mr. Forbes Glennie.

A little further on we arrive at Chapel House, so named because many years ago it was a Nonconformist Place of worship, but long since converted into a private residence and now let on lease. Almost opposite Chapel House are the cottages and trim gardens of the Thorpeness coastguard station, where, acting on the representations of the Company, the G.P.O. have opened a telegraph office (receipt and delivery) for "Thorpeness." The road then turns abruptly to the right and, bringing us back to the Kursaal, completes the circuit of the Township.

This bare recital of the position and character of the various groups of public buildings, houses and bungalows which form the nucleus of the ever-growing township, must of necessity completely fail to convey the peculiar charm and magnetic lure of Thorpeness, still less the infinite art which has been exercised in effecting an amazing transformation while yet preserving the inherent soul and character of the locality. It seems but yesterday that Thorpeness was a scattered handful of fishermen's huts and cottages lost in a waste of dunes and denes, with

THORPENESS SAND DUNES.

tussocks of bent grass gleaming in greens and silvers against the blues and yellows of sea and sand. The sea poppy and the sea thistle and the sea pea were the only flowers in Neptune's garden. To-day there has arisen a miniature township providing for almost every conceivable form of holiday recreation and distraction, yet each building seems part and parcel of the place, set there to enhance and emphasise the natural beauties of the spot. Neptune's garden remains unspoilt.

"Esther though in robes, is Esther still."

Nor has the practical side of a garden township been sacrificed in striving after æsthetic effect. Attention has already been called to the great care shown in the setting out of the township to leave ample space in every direction for gardens, orchards and plantations and the free admission of sunlight and sea air. There are three further practical points which have been dealt with in a manner that differentiates Thorpeness from many of her sister bungalow towns. The Company have seen that the Town, even in these early days, shall be provided with a safe and powerful illuminant, a particularly pure water supply and a sanitation service of the first order.

ACETYLENE GAS. Perceiving from the first that no village now-a-days could claim to be ideal which depended upon the smoky, smelly and exceedingly dangerous oil lamp for its illuminant, the Company entered into a contract with the Leading Light Syndicate, Ltd., to erect a central generating station with a 500-light installation, capable of being immediately increased to 1,000 or more lights (as and when required) and lay mains, with branch service pipes, to everyone of their houses.

These well-known Acetylene gas experts were also to provide shilling-in-the-slot meters, gas rings, with atmospheric Bunsen burners and ovens. Thorpeness has, therefore, the distinction of being the first township in Great Britain to be equipped throughout with these apparatuses.

Acetylene gas has many advantages. It is cheaper than coal gas as an illuminant, infinitely safer than oil lamps and as clean as the electric light. It cannot be too widely known or too strongly insisted upon that the proper use of Acetylene gas is not attended by any special danger. It is in actual fact safer than any other form of artificial lighting. The gas has a pungent smell which, in the event of a leak, causes it to be detected immediately. It takes moreover ten times as long as coal gas to fill a room of a given size and when full it is not injurious to health, as in the case of coal and other gases. The above facts have long been recognised by all the leading Fire Insurance Companies, who make no extra charge on the premium of houses insured, where the Acetylene gas is properly installed.

WATER SUPPLY. Everyone of the Company's buildings in Thorpeness is provided with its own water supply, the convenience of which is perhaps only fully realised by those who have endured the extreme discomfort of many bungalow towns where the visitors are dependent for this necessity upon their rain-water butts and the daily visit of the water carrier. The water supply for domestic use is obtained from a large new well sunk on the property recently acquired by the Company which skirts the entire Northern shores of the Meare and is known as Lakeside. The well is situated on one of the highest points of the Company's land, removed from the township and from all areas of possible contamination in years to come. A powerful windmill of the American type has been erected upon an elongated iron frame over the well, and provided with four large reservoir tanks to insure against the failure of wind power for 48 hours —a contingency which, having regard to the elevated and exposed position of the mill and the breezy character

THE NEW MILL.

of the East coast, may be considered extremely remote. Indeed throughout the long spell of hot and calm weather last August, there was not a single day without wind enough to work the pumps. These pumps, which can also be worked by manual labour, are capable, under normal conditions, of lifting over 10,000 gallons of water per diem.

This water has been analysed by Mr. W. Lincolne Sutton, the County Analyst, and officially declared of a peculiarly high standard of purity, as the following certificate will show:—

Norfolk and Suffolk County Laboratories,
Redwell Street,
NORWICH.

June 11th, 1913.

No. 15,189. Book P.

Sample received from H. Kemp, Esq., Estate office, Aldringham. Secretary "Seaside Bungalows Ltd.,"

Mark or seal: No. 1, New well.

Physical characteristics.	Grains per gallon.
Free Ammonia	·0016
Albumenoid ammonia	·0063
Nitrogen in nitrates	1·372
Nitrites	trace
Chlorine in chlorides	4·90
Solids in solution dried at 212 F.	26·60
Oxygen absorbed in 4 hours at 80 F.	...
Poisonous metals	...
Hardness before boiling	8·2
ditto after boiling	7·2

Remarks: This water is free from pollution and fit for drinking and general domestic purposes. Its hardness is very moderate for the district.

(Signed) W. LINCOLNE SUTTON.

SANITATION. Determined to avoid the grave errors in sanitation which have been made in more than one carelessly-created bungalow village, the Company has paid the closest attention to this question, with which the future health and reputation of Thorpeness must necessarily be identified. The latest scientific principle of antiseptic segregation has been adopted. All closets, whether using the "Sanitas" or "Moule's" principle of earth closet, are regularly attended to and disinfected twice a week by the Company's staff.

The Kursaal, the Dolphin hotel, and all the Lakeside houses are furnished with W.C.'s and cesspool drainage, carefully trapped and ventilated in strict accordance with recognised rules.

CHAPTER III.
THE KURSAAL.
(Opened by Sir Wm. Bull, M.P., May 6th, 1912.)

"To touch and go and to and fro
To gossip, talk and tattle,
To hear the news and to amuse
One's world with endless prattle."

W. W. Story.

PERHAPS the wisest—certainly the most original—step the Company has as yet taken in the development of Thorpeness was to select the best site and sea view on the Estate and erect thereon a handsome, commodious Club-house, before a single bungalow was commenced. Prospective visitors to Thorpeness were thus not asked, as is the case in so many embryo townships, to take things on trust. A peculiarly attractive social and athletic rendezvous awaited the first arrivals. The Club-house stands upon the highest point of the sand dunes facing South-east. A wide and unbroken view of the North sea is thereby obtained from the spacious balcony and from all the windows in the front of the Club-house. A similar balcony on the opposite side of the building, much affected for afternoon teas, looks out over the tennis courts, croquet lawn and bowling green and the gay borders of the flower garden.

In the North wing, besides ample kitchen and store accommodation, which are approached by the Tradesmen's entrance screened from the rest of the ground by the natural lift of the sand dunes to the North, are the usual offices and the bureau. The centre part of the building forms the lounge, 30 feet by 18 feet—where the daily papers and writing facilities are to be found and

THORPENESS~KURSAAL.

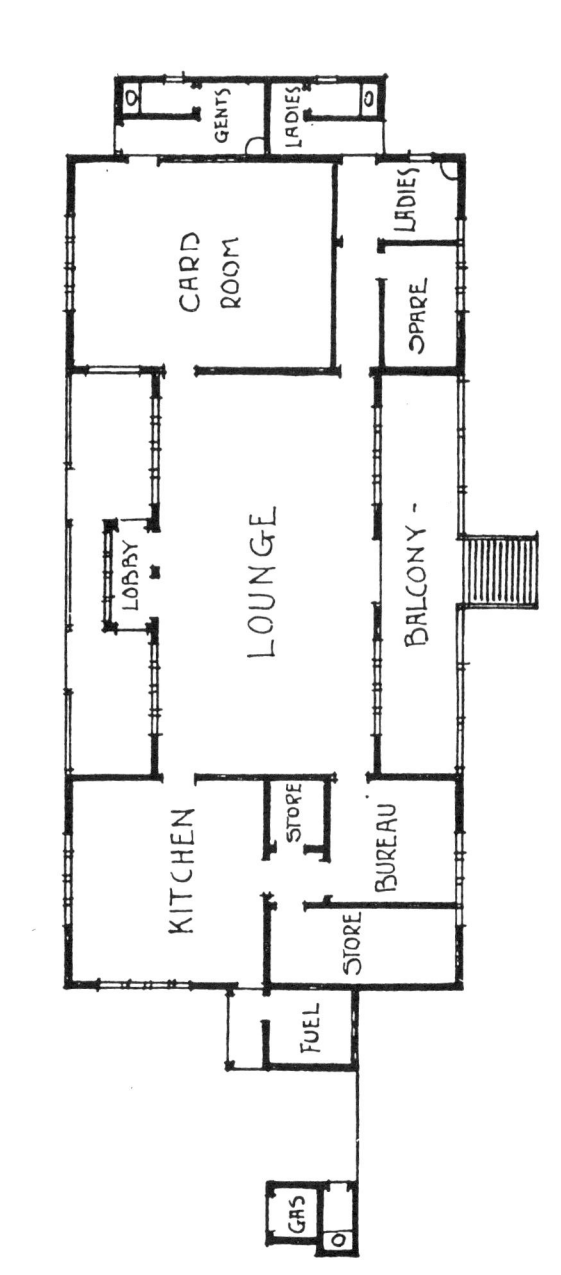

Ground Floor Plan.

(Gentlemen's Dressing Room, Bicycle Stand, and General Stores in the under-croft, not shown).

innumerable occasional tables can be set as desired for tea or for refreshments. The double set of windows looking seaward and over the playing grounds make this a peculiarly cheerful Summer pavilion. In the South

A CORNER OF THE KURSAAL.

wing, is the card room with its big bay window overlooking the sea and double glass doors giving on to the Balcony. Beyond the card room are the men's lavatories. To the West, approached by a separate passage from the lounge, are the ladies' tiring rooms and other conveniences. By a very simple and ingenious arrangement, the entire South wing, with the exception of the attendants' room and the ladies' tiring room, can be thrown into the main hall, giving a dancing floor 48 feet 6 inches long by 18 feet wide and a most convenient bay for the location of the band; or, by another equally simple arrangement, the main hall can be converted into a bijou theatre or concert hall, with dressing rooms for both sexes, and a stage 14 feet in depth from footlights to backcloth.

The space available in the undercroft is cleverly utilised to provide an ample dressing room for men (close to the tennis courts); a shelter for bicycles; large cellarage; and storage accommodation for the complex paraphernalia of a sports club. The building is lit by Acetylene gas. The original installation, including its supplementary gas rings which proved an invaluable complement to the cooking apparatus of the kitchen, worked without a single hitch and gave entire satisfaction throughout the whole of the first season. When the more ambitious system of lighting the whole township with Acetylene was adopted, the original plant was removed en bloc to the Sizewell estates, where it is used to light the fine old Elizabethan house of Scott's Hall and its extensive dairy with complete success. The Club owns a circulating library, a carefully selected cellar of wines, spirits and liqueurs, together with a complete refreshment service, which makes a speciality of its afternoon teas.

Under these circumstances it is hardly surprising that the Kursaal has already proved an exceedingly popular institution not only with the visitors and inhabitants of Thorpeness, but with many of the leading residents within a wide radius of the Club. These County members frequently motor in for tea and other refreshments, as well as to enjoy the splendid sands and sea bathing which Thorpeness alone affords. The Club has a series of portable Dhoolie bathing cabins specially invented and constructed to take the place of the old-fashioned, unwieldy bathing machines of other days.

DHOOLIE BATHING CABIN.

Mr. Forbes Glennie's ingenious construction, whereby the whole upper floor of the building, with the exception of the offices, can be converted into a concert hall, has been alluded to above. Concerts organised by the Entertainment Committee of the Club and the Thorpeness Philharmonic Society were attended by large and appreciative audiences, the accommodation of the hall, capable of seating some 240 persons, being frequently tested to its uttermost.

The Pleasure grounds of the Club are laid out on the West front and lie warm and sheltered under the lea of the sand dunes to the East. The slopes of these dunes have been utilised to form a stadium or series of com-

THORPENESS KURSAAL E.T.C. TENNIS COURTS.

fortable seats arranged in tiers overlooking the tennis courts. The latter are enclosed with high wire netting carried upon ornamental iron standards. There are at present two of these double tennis courts laid down by the well-known En Tout Cas Co. Special provision has been made whereby these courts can be quickly and thoroughly watered during droughty weather by a specially-designed apparatus operating from mains laid on either side of the courts. Although played upon continually from morning until late evening and despite the wear and tear of two public tournaments which were held during last season, these courts never failed to give complete satisfaction and were indeed so popular, that a considerable number of seaside visitors staying at Aldeburgh joined the Club in order to avail themselves of these courts—the Club-house being within easy distance of about a mile-and-a-half's pleasant walk along the sea front from that fashionable town.

Dealing with the all-important question of the advantages of the hard court over the grass court, a peculiarly interesting article appeared in "The Times" of October 1st, 1912, headed "The Coming of the Hard Court." Inasmuch as, at the opening of the Club, there appeared to be a disposition, in certain quarters, to question the wisdom of the Proprietors in building hard instead of grass courts, we feel justified in giving the following extract from this article: "For some years past Continental players have been winning lawn tennis tournaments and it is now usual to ascribe much of the credit of these victories to the hard court on which the winners received their early training. The hard court possesses some obvious advantages; it requires comparatively little tending; it can be used all the year round; and above all its service is true. It is not to be wondered at then that the number of hard courts has been steadily increasing in England, although here the hard court was regarded until recently as an under-study for the superior grass court. But this attitude seems to be changing; there must now be a considerable body of players who regard a grass court as a horse omnibus—to be used when a newer and better article is not available. The weather of the last few months has done much to strengthen this opinion. In accounts of grass court tournaments it has been a common thing to read: No progress could be made with the handicaps and it was only by using the hard courts which were laid down recently that the open events could be brought to a conclusion. And on all sides one hears of Clubs determined not to face another tournament season unprovided with hard courts."

Beyond the tennis court enclosure lies the full-sized Wimbledon croquet lawn, surrounded by a gravel path and flower borders and protected to the North and North-east by a substantial wooden fence, 6-ft. high. Under a new rule of the Club, if a sufficient number of members desire to play bowls, they are able to book the lawn for this purpose. The flower borders have been made a special feature of the pleasure grounds and the rotunda immediately in front of the West balcony is crowded each season with bright bedding-out and herbaceous plants and forms a particularly pleasing spot of colour amidst the surrounding silver and grey tones of the bent grass on the sand dunes.

CHAPTER IV.

THE MEARE.

(Opened by the Right Honble. Lord Huntingfield, June 11th, 1913).

"And its lakes were all of the dazzling sheen,
Like magic mirrors, where slumbering lay
The sun, and the sky, and the cloudlet grey."
James Hogg.

THE geographical and seignorial history of the Meare has already been given under another chapter, but this bare statement of facts conveys little or no idea of the absolute transformation which has been accomplished, at the cost of several thousands of pounds, by the Company, in the landscape to the South-west of the township. A veritable Suffolk broad has been created, and the Company justly claim that there is no sheet of water nearer than the famous Norfolk broads which can offer such an ideal lake for the recreation of adults and children alike. This ornamental water, covering an area of over 61 acres, and confined by more than 4 miles of embankment, has one particular characteristic which makes it probably absolutely unique as a "playground" for the young. Except in one or two places which have been suitably protected, the maximum depth of the water does not exceed 2 feet 6 inches. Children may, therefore, be safely trusted to roam thereon alone, without fear of any mishap other than a possible ducking.

At the North-east corner of the lake facing the Village green stands the Club boat-house, which is approached by a circular sweep from the Aldringham and Thorpe road opposite the Haven bungalows. The main entrance close to the clock tower, which is a striking feature of the East elevation, admits members through an open porch on to a spacious estrade and loggia looking Westward, and facing the full extent of the lake and its islands. To the left of the entrance are dressing rooms and lavatory accommodation for both sexes, and the bureau or booking office. On the right are the kitchen and service offices, while overhead is a commodious cottage for the Waterman and Stewardess of the Club. Below the estrade is a wide landing-stage, which is continued Northward beyond the Club building for the benefit of those members of the public who are not members of the Club and yet desire to hire some form of boat. The loggia is supplied with chairs and tables, and forms a particularly pleasant lounge for tea or other refreshments. During last season this loggia was thrown open to non-members desiring to take tea between the hours of 4 and 6 p.m. Large numbers of the residents and visitors to Aldeburgh availed themselves of this privilege, as many as 30 and 40 teas being frequently served to such visitors during the afternoon and it is proposed to continue this concession until further notice.

The Club-house, which is a sort of *dependence* of the Kursaal (annual members of the latter being at present honorary members of the former), has been primarily established for the benefit of seaside visitors at Aldeburgh and for residents in the locality who desire all the convenience of a Club-house while giving their children an outing on these waters. The management of the

THE BOAT CLUB CLUB-HOUSE—WEST VIEW.

Club is in the hands of the Committee and of Mr. Graeme Kemp, Secretary. Sir Frederick Adair, Bart., honoured the Club by consenting to become the first President, while amongst the names of the Vice-Presidents we notice those of Major-General Sir Ronald Lane, K.C.V.O., C.B., Captain Vernon-Wentworth, R.N., and Frank Garrett, Esq., junior.

The subscriptions for those members who are not annual members of the Kursaal are framed upon the principle of the *abonnement* of a Continental casino, viz., for each adult person 10/- per annum, 5/- per month, 1/- per day; children under 12 being admitted at half-price. Family tickets, including all members of a particular family or party, are issued at special rates. Special terms are also quoted for school outings.

A large fleet of rowing boats, including skiffs, prams, and dingheys, together with canoes and Thames punts, are for hire, while a squadron of Una-rigged centre-boards, built by Mr. A. Everson, of Woodbridge, specially constructed for the class of water on which they are to be used, are available for sailing purposes. A peculiar and picturesque feature of this squadron is that each boat is not only provided with a stimulating and romantic name—such as "The Red Rover," "The Yellow Peril," "The Black Prince," "The Blue Bird," "The Purple Emperor," "The Brown Bear," "The Pink Pearl," &c., &c.—but is furnished with a different coloured mainsail to accord with its name. The effect of these many-coloured sails flitting about this inland sea, almost as blue and quite as tideless as the Mediterranean itself, presents a really remarkable and striking picture. No little skill is required in handling these flat-bottomed cat-boats under a fresh South-Westerly breeze, as various shoals and shallows have been purposely left in certain portions of the lake which necessitate a quick and clever manipulation of the centre-board, and may well lead to the capsizing of the unwary if the wind is at all squally, to the great joy, no doubt, of his more cunning companions under sail. In short, to the average citizen with an amateur's taste for rowing or sailing, or as a follower of, perhaps, the most graceful of all aquatic exercises—punting—the Meare with its wide expanse, its varied tree-planted islands, and its quiet nooks and reed-grown back-waters, forms an absolutely ideal arena for healthy exercise or the lazy dreaming of a Summer's afternoon. Indeed the instantaneous popular success of this new and only Suffolk broad has altogether exceeded the most sanguine expectations of the Company. Although the lake was only opened about the middle of June, 1913, and despite the fact that July was wet and unfavourable for boating, over 7,500 persons availed themselves of the facilities offered for rowing, sailing and punting on these waters up to November 1st when the Meare was redrained to permit of further structural enlargements and embellishments.

The fleet of 40 boats, which has now been largely augmented, frequently proved insufficient for the demand. A motor-boat has been added to this fleet and will be on hire for private parties (with attendance) and also make public trips round the lake during holiday times. But it was perhaps to the little folk that the Meare made its strongest appeal last season. Allowed to range the entire extent of this vast inland sea by themselves, unhampered by the presence and control of their elders, many of the children at Thorpeness seemed to spend their entire holiday on or about these waters. The Magic Pavilion was in great vogue and constantly hired by parents for pic-nic and tea parties. A large business was done in sweets, ærated waters, etc., at Wendy's House, while the Pirates' Lair, the Brigands' Haunt, Roaring Camp and the Smugglers' Cave were visited daily by crowds of juvenile visitors. The new Island, with Peggotty's Hut thereon, will be sure to command equally extensive patronage this year. A full account of the Meare as "The Children's Paradise" is given in Chapter V.

An impromptu Regatta, held on August Bank holiday, proved a very popular attraction. The same evening an *al fresco* Concert on the water opposite the Magic Pavilion drew hundreds of people to the reserved seats on the island which was illuminated by Acetylene search lights, and, favoured by a singularly still and starlit night, the entertainment was admitted on all sides to have been both unique and fascinating.

A Venetian fête was held in connection with the annual Thorpeness marine regatta, when prizes were offered for the best decorated and illuminated boats. The effect of the Club, Wendy's House and the Magic Pavilion decorated and defined by myriads of fancy lights, of the many coloured Chinese lanterns on the water and of the fireworks across the lake which concluded the fête will long be remembered by those who were fortunate enough to witness this beautiful scene.

MODEL YACHT RACING.

For those, and there are many, who are interested in the sailing of model yachts or the running of model motor boats, the Haven Bay, surrounded as it is on three sides by the semi-circular Barrie's Walk, affords an ideal racing ground.

FISHING.

A considerable area to the North-west of the Meare has been specially wired off, and stocked with carp, golden orfe, roach and other coarse fish. Two interesting cases of fish, caught in the Meare, are displayed in the loggia of the Boat-house, viz., a golden orfe weighing 2-lbs. 4-ozs., and a Prussian carp weighing 3-lbs. 4-ozs. Another orfe extracted from the Preserve (unfortunately by a predatory and poaching Heron) weighed over $2\frac{1}{2}$-lbs., while it is reported that a third orfe has been frequently seen, of prodigious dimensions, and far larger than any fish already captured. The above specimens were preserved and mounted by Mr. T. E. Gunn, the famous Norwich taxidermist. There are one or two deep and rather dangerous holes, apparently of the same formation as the well-known Pulk holes on the Norfolk broads, within this enclosure, which is the only place on the Meare where children will not be permitted, unless attended by someone in charge. Terms to fish these private waters can be obtained from the Secretary of the Boat Club.

WILD FOWLING.

Fifty years ago the Thorpe Meare was famous throughout the county for its wild fowl and there are several inhabitants of the old fishing village still alive who can testify to the record bags of swans, geese, duck, teal, widgeon and other wild fowl made by the local gunners in those days. Since the re-flooding of the Meare, the duck have again come in from the sea in great numbers and there is every reason to believe that this wide stretch of water, with its reedlands and other shelter, will, when properly preserved, once more become one of the best Winter fowling grounds on the Suffolk coast. Although, as stated above, the water was run off during the whole of the Winter, several good bags of wild duck were obtained and two wild swans weighing 20 and 21 lbs. respectively were shot on the Meare last season. For permits to shoot, application may be made to the Secretary of the Boat Club.

It should perhaps be mentioned that it was the original intention of the Company to reflood the Meare by admitting the sea through a shore sluice. After much careful consideration this scheme was abandoned, chiefly for horticultural reasons, as the introduction of salt water would have made any attempt at planting trees, reeds, or other vegetation on the banks and fringes of the lake and its islands a certain and foregone failure.

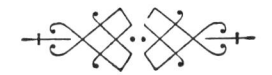

CHAPTER V.

THE CHILDREN'S PARADISE.

"If Sailor tales to Sailor tunes,
Storm and adventure, heat and cold,
If schooners, islands and maroons
And Buccaneers and buried gold,
And all the old Romance re-told
Exactly in the ancient way,
Can please, as me they pleased of old,
The wiser youngsters of to-day—
So be it and fall on."
Robert Louis Stevenson.

IN creating the Meare, with its rush-encircled and tree-crowned islands, out of the sodden and dreary mud flats of other days, the Company has provided scope for perpetual adventure to all those of either sex who are still young enough at heart to enter into the joyous spirit of a children's holiday.

Let the stuffy elders, an they choose, haste to the yellow sands or the heather lands, or the Kursaal to play croquet or tennis, or doze over the illustrated papers on the sunny balcony. We, the Adventurers, have other more desperate business on hand and make a bee-line for the lake. If we come from afar, either by motor or carriage, we approach the Boat-house by the new road branching from the Aldringham and Thorpeness road opposite the Haven bungalows, where we leave our vehicle in the convenient shelter adjacent to the Club. Or, if we hail from the opposite direction of Aldeburgh, we can easily walk or comfortably drive either by public conveyance or our own carriage, to the Jubilee bridge, after which we must proceed at a foot-pace over about a quarter-mile of sandy un-metalled track till we reach the Village Green. It was an amazing sight last season to see strings of motors of all sizes and makes fearlessly and cheerfully negotiating these uninviting paths.

The landing stage for non-members of the Club lies to the North of the building and the waterman is summoned by the clanging of a large bell at one corner of the landing stage. We, however, mean to miss none of the fun and have already engaged by letter or telegram, (for the somewhat modest sum of half-a-crown) an island "for our very own property own" which carries with it the privilege of day membership for our entire party. Proceeding therefore with a certain air of importance through the main entrance, we march straight for the bureau on the left. Here we are confronted by the Pirate King, a stern-faced man wearing a truculent blood-red cap. As we speak him fair, he offers us no violence, but leads us—even with a certain show of courtesy—to the boat or boats or even the exciting "Gee-Whiz" motor launch which we have also, if wise, engaged beforehand. The little tea tables which stand dotted about the loggia do not tempt us, for we are bent upon refreshment under more romantic—if less comfortable — conditions, and we therefore make a careful selection of the necessary paraphernalia for our island tea party. This important collection, which can be hired for a small sum from the waterman at the Club, will certainly comprise an iron tripod, a kettle, a bundle of fuel, and, if we are wise, a small

THE GEE-WHIZ AND HER CAP'N.

packet of potatoes which we intend to roast — and burn our fingers with—later on. If we have not bought our own tea, milk, hot water, cakes, and the homely but necessary *tartine*, these too can be purchased from the Stewardess of the Club. We then, with considerable fussation and much shouting of contradictory orders, having victualled our good ships, stow ourselves more or less unsafely therein, and push forth upon the vasty deep. We are probably plying the busy oar, because even if there is a welcome breeze, the handling of a Una-rigged cat-boat, with children as our crew, invites a damp calamity before we reach our first port of call.

The Captain of each boat has of course purchased a Chart to the Children's Paradise (involving the heavy outlay of one penny), for without this mysterious and monstrous map we should indeed be as a ship without its rudder upon this magic sea. And so, for a good hour or more we pursue our fearless but erratic voyage of exploration across the whole extent of the Meare, recalling the familiar lines of that arch-lover of all children, *Lewis Carroll* :—

> "All in the golden afternoon,
>   Full leisurely we glide,
> For both our oars, with little skill,
>   By little arms are plied,
> While little hands make vain pretence
>   Our wanderings to guide."

It is fair to say that Billy Bones, the reputed author of the chart, appears to have been no precise cartographer and although he has marked in many of the leading features of the Meare with a rough exactitude, there are certain grave geographical omissions in his "ordinance of land and water." For instance the Hard has now entirely disappeared—possibly owing to some volcanic or seismic convulsion—and furthermore, Mr. Bones, in his wanderings apparently never reached the North Pole or risked his life by attempting to force the North-west Passage, a wide channel which runs behind the Dismal Swamp round the entire North-west margin of the Meare till it reaches the Fairway hard by the Sunset Isles of Boshen.

If we intend to faithfully make the *tour du lac*—over two miles in length—we shall head South-west for the River of Years, which runs between the Pampas (with its Playing Fields) and The Kingdom of the Future, into the Caribbean sea. Hugging the shore of these wild waters and keeping Deadman's creek and the World's end on our larboard quarter, we set our course due North to Wendy's house, where perchance we may supplement our earlier victualling with butter scotch, chocolate, lemonade and other marine stores. Thence we again cross the Spanish main, pass Coral island—sacred to the memory of gallant Masterman Ready—and skirt the uncharted coast of Lakeside, till we strike the North-west passage, which leads us through the Devil's dyke (where we keep our weather-eye lifting for the crocodile) into Lake Pipple-Popple. Here we pass through the Gateway of Dreams and find ourselves at last in the Blue Lagoon, The Children's Paradise, the heart and home of all our make-believe. And surely we must be of the Very Unhappies who were born old if we cannot assimilate ourselves to this atmosphere of the little folks' romance. If we are boys, and, therefore, of a blood-thirsty and dare-devil disposition, we must carefully consider upon what particular class of battle, murder and sudden death we are about to embark. To some the Brigand's Haunt with its solitary gun, squat and vicious-looking, peeking from its gnarled and tangled zareba of tree trunks, will call; others may select the red-tinted Roaring Camp, with its two miniature cannon resting on the low encircling rampart; others may prefer the damp and murky interior of The Smuggler's Cave, half-hidden from the lake by its surrounding jungle of tall bulrushes. But probably, if we are really truculent, Byronic corsairs, the Pirates' Lair will most attract, with its amazing fort dominating the lake crowned by a flagstaff (on which, with due and awful ceremony, we may hoist the Jolly Roger borrowed from the Pirate King on starting) and bristling at its various embrasures with historic artillery "Mons Meg," "Malek è Maidan" (Lord of the Plains),

THE PIRATE KING AND LITTLE BILL-EE.

and "Long Tom." Here we will light our fire, boil our Camp billy, blacken our faces, burn our fingers and probably our clothes and generally have the time of our life.

But if we are girls, who may be voted dull by the boy brigade as being too squeamish in our blood-letting, we will leave these desperadoes to their fell intent and take refuge in the Magic Pavilion, situated on Fay Island and overshadowed by the Tulgy wood. For here the Little Mistress of our party can hold high court, and play the Little Mother and the Very Perfect Housewife, undisturbed by rude and brutal boys. And lo! within this most magic of Magic Pavilions, with its silver roof, and its wicked-looking yellow and red stripes outside, we find, besides a real drawing-room with real mirrors, real curtains, and (more or less) real jewels, a real kitchen with a real stove, where real eggs can be poached, and a real and glorious mess made of ourselves and everything. Or if we have been brought up in the new and horrid

LITTLE EM'LY AT PEGGOTTY'S HOUSE.

school which teaches that Fairy Stories are demoralizing and The Pari-Banou a fib, we may prefer to engage Peggotty's Hut with its funny old walls of turf, its funny wee windows and door and its funny shaped cabin inside made out of a big black boat turned upside down just like that other house where "Mas'r Davy" played with "Little Em'ly" in the days of long ago.

Thus, full of happy entertainment and great imaginings, wherever we may be, the hours slip by till the Westering summer sun begins to cast long shadows across the Meare, and warns us that we must collect the various details of our happy army and re-embark. And so, very dirty and very tired, and perhaps a little fractious, but supremely content, we return to the Boat-house from whence we came, with set determination of very shortly repeating our happy experiences in The Children's Paradise.

CHAPTER VI.
COMMUNICATIONS WITH THORPENESS

POSTAL FACILITIES.—The business of the Post-office is at present conducted on the premises of the Thorpeness stores, a temporary building erected opposite "The Dolphin" Hotel, pending the building of the series of shops in the Rows. There is a morning and afternoon delivery and collection of letters.

TELEGRAPH.—A receiving and delivery office has been opened at the Coastguard station. Telegraphic address: "Thorpeness."

TELEPHONE. Arrangements have been made with the General Post Office to lay the telephone into the Kursaal Club-house if, and when, desired, but at present it seems to be the wish of the majority of the members, especially amongst the business members of the Club, that telephonic communication with Thorpeness should not be established there, but anyone desiring to telephone may do so from the Estate office near the Boat Club-house.

MOTOR ROADS. — The only good road by which Thorpeness can at present be reached is by the road from Aldringham. Motors can, however, and frequently do travel from Aldeburgh over the Jubilee bridge and the intervening quarter-mile of unmetalled cart tracks.

to the Boat-club at Thorpeness. An effort has been made to induce the Corporation of Aldeburgh to improve this carriage road, and extend it from the bridge to the boundary of their district. We are further informed that Capt. Wentworth, the Lord of the Manor of Aldeburgh, has generously promised to present the Corporation with the necessary width of land where the road runs through his property from the Jubilee Bridge to the said boundary, while the Directors of SEASIDE BUNGALOWS LTD. are prepared to continue this road at their own expense from that boundary to the Aldringham road. Although we understand that the Aldeburgh Corporation do not see their way to carrying out their share of this means of communication between Aldeburgh and Thorpeness this year, it is hoped that the completion of the road, which would confer many mutual advantages, cannot be long postponed, as it would afford the means of an interesting circular drive for visitors to both places, which is not now possible.

RAILWAY SERVICE.—The Great Eastern Railway have extended their privileges of cheap seaside week-end, tourist and other tickets to Leiston (for Thorpeness), as well as Aldeburgh. As all trains on the branch line stop at Leiston station, visitors at Thorpeness enjoy the full benefit of the admirable Summer quick seaside service of the G.E.R. to and from Aldeburgh. By using a motor from Leiston, any Railway traveller to Thorpeness can actually reach his front door earlier than an Aldeburgh visitor can arrive at his home by the same train. The means of closer communication between our ever-growing Garden City by the sea and the G.E.R. has, naturally, had the Company's very serious attention. Such a problem necessarily raises the difficult and delicate question of how to preserve the secluded and select character of Thorpeness, while affording residents and visitors easy accessibility to the outer world.

We understand that correspondence has passed between the Company and the courteous General Manager of the G.E.R., and that the latter Company are prepared at any time to erect and open a "Halt" at or near the level crossing on the Thorpeness and Aldringham road,

SITE OF FUTURE RAILWAY STATION.

upon certain fair and even liberal conditions. It may be taken for granted that such a halt will certainly be established before the future Golf Links are open to the public. In the interim, a subsidiary Company promoted by Seaside Bungalows Ltd., under the title of Thorpeness Vitesse, Ltd., has been registered. Vitesse, Ltd., runs two covered-in Daimler cars and meets any G.E.R. train at Leiston by appointment. This Company also runs a somewhat novel form of motor train, the tractor being one of the above-mentioned 38 H.P. Daimler cars specially converted for the purpose by gearing down with an enlarged chain ring containing 54 teeth instead of the standard No. of 42. This tractor is fitted with a wagonette body which is surmounted by a weather-proof canvas covering, and side roller blinds, and holds 11 passengers and the driver. Attached to the trailer by a spring buffer link is a chassis, carrying a double-deck 'bus and capable of accommodating some 30 passengers, the front part of the chassis being provided with a van for heavy luggage and parcels.

This train ran continually during last season on Sundays, Bank and other holidays, between Leiston and Thorpeness, frequently carrying over 40 passengers each journey without a single failure or mishap, which, as there are three hills to negotiate, says no little for the endurance and reserve power of the Daimler motor.

CHAPTER VII.

THE ECONOMICS OF THORPENESS.

"Though on pleasure she was bent
She had a frugal mind."
Cowper.

WE have tried to deal in the foregoing pages with the architectural, æsthetic, recreative, sanitary and domestic aspects of Thorpeness as it is at present and will be in the future when the township has reached its final development. The last word should, perhaps, be rightly devoted to the Economic side of this new and unique holiday resort. The housing accommodation has been carefully designed to suit all purses, ranging from the modest cottages fully furnished, and with gas and water laid on, at 2 guineas, to the luxurious Lakeside residences with bath rooms and all modern conveniences, large gardens running down to the lake, etc., at 15 guineas per week.

It should be particularly noted that in every case where any house of the Company is taken on lease, the rent covers all and every charge except Acetylene gas, which illuminant is supplied at a rate some 10% below that charged for coal gas in any neighbouring town or similar seaside place. *There are no extras.* When the tenant has paid his rent, he knows exactly what his liabilities are. The rent quoted covers all rates including the water rate), taxes, repairs (other than breakages and damage), sanitary attendance, and even the upkeep and stocking of the flower garden, including lawn cutting and rolling, sweeping and the provision of herbaceous or bedding-out plants for the season. This system of one over-all charge has proved particularly popular and probably accounts for so very large a percentage of the Company's houses having been taken for a term of years—many of them before the roof was on. If the above facts are taken into consideration, the rents at Thorpeness will be found to be from 15 to 20% lower than at any other seaside resort of equal standing and with equal advantages on the East coast.

The numerous recreations and diversions offered to visitors or residents at Thorpeness are provided on an equally economical scale of charges. Indeed the Company justly claims that there is no other seaside holiday town in Great Britain that offers so many and such varied distractions within so small a radius and at so nominal a price. For instance, the subscription to the Kursaal is one guinea per annum or $1\frac{1}{2}$ guineas for husband and wife. There is at present no entrance fee. The terms of subscription to the Boat Club have already been quoted (p. 67). The subscription to the Playing Fields is equally low. An inclusive monthly "omnibus" ticket is issued by the Company to the tenants of all their houses, admitting all members of one family or household to all the Company's Clubs and grounds at a specially reduced rate. Such tickets admit the nominated bearers to the Kursaal and all its privileges, to the Boathouse, to the Playing Fields and the Pavilion, and permit the free use of the tennis courts, croquet lawn, bowling green, clock golf green, rounders ground and stump cricket pitch. Such tickets further entitle the holders to the sole use of any available boat upon the Meare at the reduced rate of 30/- per month for the months of August or September, or 15/- for any other month in the year.

The Company have been able to quote this abnormally low tariff and still leave a reasonable margin of profit to themselves by obtaining, with no little forethought, a combined and co-operative control of every necessary detail of a complete building estate, aided by low local rates. The expense of one central office and Directorate only has to be met. The land, the buildings and the entire water supply, as well as the very recreation grounds, ornamental lake, fleet of boats, and Clubs are managed by one control, with the consequence that each department is designed to co-operate with, rather than compete against, the undertaking as a whole.

LEASE OF BUILDING SITES.

In response to numerous enquiries received last year from persons desirous of erecting their own houses at Thorpeness, the Company are prepared to lease building sites of various sizes and in various positions on the Estate. A very few sites are still available on the sea front and a considerable number on Lakeside and in other portions of the Township. The leases granted will be subject to protective conditions as regards the size and quality of buildings and their external appearance, as well as sanitation, the planting and laying out of the gardens, etc., etc., so that the picturesque and practical features of Thorpeness shall be maintained at their present high standard. All plans will have to be submitted to and passed by the Managing Director and the Estate Architect. The Company will arrange to lay on and supply their gas and water to such houses as may be built under these leases, at a reasonable rate.

CHAPTER VIII.
"AS ITHERS SEE US."

> "Yet doth he give us bold Advertisement,
> That with our small conjunction we should on,
> To see how fortune is disposed to us."
> *Shakespeare.*

It is impossible in the limited space of this Guide to publish in full the many lengthy and flattering notices which have appeared in all the leading London newspapers and in many of the chief provincial journals concerning Thorpeness.

The following necessarily brief and curtailed quotations will give some faint idea of how our Garden village by the sea strikes the interested visitor:

LONDON PAPERS.

The Times.

"Thorpeness Meare, the latest development in connection with the bungalow village, was yesterday opened by LORD HUNTINGFIELD. At one corner of the lake is a large Club boat-house and many islands have been picturesquely named after spots mentioned in the works of SIR J. M. BARRIE, R. L. STEVENSON, and LEWIS CARROLL .... MR. STUART OGILVIE, presiding at the opening ceremony, said he hoped they were assisting in the inauguration of what would develop in a few years into one of the beauty spots of Suffolk. LORD HUNTINGFIELD then declared the Meare open, specially alluding to the advantages of having a safe, shallow lake for children."

The Daily Telegraph.

"NEW EAST COAST RESORT. Town-planning inland has been very popular of late, but the designing of an ideal seaside village has not been attempted hitherto. If such a holiday haunt could be created it would surely be on the East coast, where there are unlimited sea breezes and sunshine as all-important accessories, and a wealth of yellow beaches and vacant land to experiment with .... Thorpeness, a little fishing village a mile-and-a-half on the Southwold side of Aldeburgh, is, in fact, a combination of cottages and bungalows, pitched here and there among the sand dunes. Situated on the outskirts of lovely heathland, it is an excellent spot for an unconventional holiday .... Now a veritable Suffolk broad has been created .... Its many islands and miniature fjiords have received names dear to the traditions of every nursery, and this must make it still more attractive. Altogether, with its breezy sands, quaint but convenient bungalows, and fine air, Thorpeness ought to have its full share of popularity in common with the other nineteen kindred towns served by the Great Eastern Railway on the Norfolk and Suffolk coasts."

The Standard.

"Thorpeness possesses the only shilling-in-the-slot acetylene installation to be found in England. A shilling commands twenty hours of gas for cooking purposes and forty hours for lighting."

The Evening Standard.

"An increasing tendency is noticeable on the part of holiday-makers to seek out secluded spots where, free from the noise and bustle of town life, they may rest their nerves. Among retreats of this class few are more worthy of a visit than Thorpeness, a little village by the sea, near Aldeburgh, in Suffolk, which has just been considerably developed."

Morning Post.

"There are three dozen bungalows facing the North sea, with only the smoke of a passing steamer to disturb the horizon. Behind the row of timber houses lies a Meare, sixty acres in extent, and only two feet deep. The Meare is, indeed, the home of Peter Pan. You take one of the little boats, with green, or brown or purple sails, and in a few minutes you are scudding across the 'blue lagoon,' running under the guns of the 'fort,' from which flies the Jolly Roger, and slipping down the creek to the 'pirates lair'."

Daily News & Leader.

"DELIGHTFUL PLAYGROUND ON THE SUFFOLK COAST. The home of Peter Pan has been found. On the Suffolk coast, just North of Aldeburgh, lies the little village of Thorpeness .... Yesterday the Meare, refilled and banked, covering 61 acres, was opened for the use of visitors by LORD HUNTINGFIELD, but with a glory that old days never knew. Its surface is studded with tiny islets where Peter Pan and Wendy have their homes .... On another island is a 'Smugglers' Cave,' built of turf with rough benches inside and a candle lantern hanging in the roof. It has its gipsy kettle on a tripod hanging over a real open-air fire. 'Roaring Camp' is another delightful spot, and the water all round is only two feet at its greatest depth."

Daily Express.

"Thorpeness, near Aldeburgh, is leading the way in the model bungalow town movement championed by the Seaside Bungalows Company, Limited, on the East coast .... The water in the Meare is only two feet deep. It covers an area of 61 acres, and the islands, which have been laid out with smugglers' caves, forts and little magic pavilions, form an ideal setting for the schemes of children's make-believe play." (*Photograph given of Tennis in the sea at Thorpeness.*)

Daily Chronicle.

"GARDEN VILLAGE BY THE SEA. One of the newest and most attractive of seaside resorts on the bracing East Coast is Thorpeness in Suffolk, a delightful combination of bungalows and cottages set among sand dunes .... Now all is changed by Seaside Bungalows, Limited, which has planted a garden village by the sea. To the natural advantages of a long stretch of sandy beach, the Company has added a Kursaal, and, by re-flooding the old 'Meare' which had run dry, has provided a shallow 'broad' comparable in beauty to any one in Norfolk."

The Morning Advertiser.

"SUFFOLK COAST DEVELOPMENT. The latest bit of *terra incognita* to be captured from absolutely primeval wilderness by the Seaside Bungalows (Limited), is Thorpeness—a bungalow township on the golden marge of the sea ...... One of its most attractive features is the magnificent stretch of sands .... From Liverpool Street the train journey takes about 2½ hours, branching from the main line to Yarmouth at Saxmundham, and proceeding to Leiston, on the line to Aldeburgh. From Leiston it is an easy drive by road to Thorpeness .... The village already boasts of a Kursaal, numerous bungalows, a croquet ground, a bowling green, and there is 'in the air' a golf course which will relieve the congested links at Aldeburgh."

Pall Mall Gazette.

"Thorpeness, the Cinderella of East Coast seaside resorts, has certainly benefited by the advent of the motor, which brings our garden village by the sea as near to London as its famous neighbour Aldeburgh, while it still remains far enough from a railway station to escape the invasion of 'nosebag trippers' .... The forty new bungalows and rustic cottages, with pure water and acetylene gas laid on to each building, are all let, mostly on lease .... At least 30 new bungalows will be built for next season."

The People.

"There is something weirdly picturesque and attractive about the sandy shores of Suffolk and Norfolk .... I am still at Thorpeness, attracted by its strange beauty, and sitting at the top of a sand dune admiring my novel surroundings and taking in the ozone by invisible bucket-loads .... Thorpeness is bound to become a very popular seaside resort, which can be easily reached by the many sumptuous restaurant trains which the Great Eastern run so frequently, making life by rail a dream of joy."

Lloyd's Weekly News.

"IDEAL RESORT FOR CHILDREN ON THE SUFFOLK COAST. A playground within sight of the sea, where children may roam and romp at will, without fear of falling over dangerous rocks or jagged cliffs; where they may wade, swim and bathe in an artificial lake, the greatest depth of which is only some 2 feet, in a district which is easily accessible to Londoners, surely must come as a boon and a blessing to parents who are always on the qui vive for a change of venue at holiday time. Such a place is Thorpeness."

The Referee.

"At Thorpeness, about a mile to the North of Aldeburgh, on the Suffolk coast, private enterprise has planted the first seeds of a little bungalow town which has many natural advantages. There is a fine stretch of sands, the surrounding country is quite attractive; and last, but most important of all, the Great Eastern Railway Company is doing all it can to encourage visitors to Thorpeness."

Town Topics.

"'What do you think of the new bungalow village or town of Thorpeness?' is a question that has been asked me by a great many people, who have not yet made themselves acquainted with this remote corner of Suffolk. I have only one opinion, and that is, if Thorpeness is carried out on the lines and to the plans I have seen, it will before very long be recognised above all others along and around the East coast as the safest, healthiest and most delightful spot for children to stay at that positively could be found."

ILLUSTRATED PAPERS.

The Sphere.

Reporting and illustrating the opening of the Kursaal at Thorpeness in its issue as far back as June 8th, 1912, "The Sphere" said: "The seaside hamlet of Thorpe, known as Thorpeness, two miles North of that most delightful of English watering-places, Aldeburgh, is on the Aldeburgh branch of the Great Eastern Railway. At present it can only be reached from Leiston Station, the station before Aldeburgh .... Thorpeness has great possibilities .... a great future before it."

Daily Mirror.

"Fighting Pirates at Peter Pan's Summer Home, Thorpeness, Suffolk, June 14th, 1913. To be transported from the dull, dusty streets round Drury lane to the Summer retreat of Peter Pan and Wendy, to pirate-infested lagoons and magic islands and smugglers' caves—that was the delightful experience of eleven tiny London boys and girls to-day .... Skirting the dense masses of reeds and bushes (in which we were told land-crabs and anacondas abounded, altho' tigers were scarce) the boats cautiously made their way past Wendy's house, towards the smugglers'

cave. Here began the serious business of the day ....
So many fights ensued, voyages of discovery, big-game
expeditions and other delightful adventures that it is impossible to record them. The slaughter among the pirates
was terrific ......" (*Photographs showing: 1, Attacking a
fort from the sea; 2, Cannon to guard against pirates; 3,
Trying to storm the fort; 4, Repelling an attack by pirates.
Further photographs were also given, in later issues, of Bathers
being carried to the sea in Dhoolie bathing machines; Rugby
football played by bathers in the Meare, etc.*)

Ladies' Field.

"Thorpeness is a garden village by the sea, with extensive
safe, beautiful sands unequalled by any on the Suffolk coast,
pretty model bungalows springing up everywhere, planted
round with sycamore, ilex, ash, oak and fir trees. Truly a
newly-discovered Eden, alike for all-the-year-round residents
and Summer holiday visitors .... Thorpeness had a
wonderful first season last Summer; it will have a splendid
one this year, being able to entertain far more visitors, who
are already applying eagerly for hotel and other accommodation. There are a delightful Kursaal and club, circulating
library, extensive sands, safe and really perfect bathing, a
superb water supply arranged on the latest scientific basis,
and public hard tennis courts that can be played on in all
weathers." (*Illustration of Thorpeness: The Boathouse on the
Meare; and Thorpeness Kursaal, with E.T.C. hard tennis courts*).

Lady's Pictorial.

"Thorpeness .... is easily reached on the G.E.R.
via Leiston .... and it reminds one very much of the
North of France watering places, at present of course on a
small scale. We know of no other place which should have
such safe attractions for young people; the air is delightful
and bracingly healthy.

Daily Sketch.
"A novel form of bathing machine is in use on the East coast at Thorpeness. It is a light construction of canvas and wood. It is so light, in fact, that it can be carried about just like a Sedan chair." (*Two large illustrations*).

Daily Graphic.
Another illustration showing Dhoolie bathing machine in operation; also a picture of Rugby football in the Meare.

Railway News.
"The Kursaal had all the conveniences of a Club, and there were excellent lawn tennis courts and a croquet and bowling green." (*Illustrations: Thorpeness, 1 The Kursaal; 2 The Boathouse; 3 Some of the bungalows*).

Great Eastern Railway Magazine.
"Thorpeness .... is at present more conveniently reached from Leiston, passengers being carried to and fro by a motor conveyance known as the "Vitesse." Contrary to the usual plan of not providing recreation rooms and facilities until a certain number of visitors is assured, a commodious and well-arranged Kursaal was erected as an initiatory part of this pleasant bungalow town, where the papers can be read, meals be obtained and games played." (*Illustrations: 1 The Boathouse and Meare; 2 The Sands; 3 The Dhoolie bathing cabin; 4 The Bungalows; 5 The Kursaal.*)

PROVINCIAL PRESS.

East Anglian Daily Times.
"The charming little seaside bungalow village of Thorpeness was throughout Wednesday in a pleasant state of excitement. The day marked the formal opening of the Meare .... Thorpeness makes its special appeal as a Summer resort .... An inspection of the bungalow town was then made and the visitors were delighted with many of the features of this novel village."

Ipswich Evening Star.

"Thus while the strenuous elders are engaged in an exciting game of tennis on the well-constructed hard courts near by the Kursaal, the juveniles, intent on high adventures of their own, will repair to this lake, row off in a boat romantically named 'the Red Rover' or 'the Blue Bird' and explore the recesses of Crusoe's island, Wendy's house, the Brigand's haunt, the Dismal Swamp or any other of the quaintly named islands of this delectable pleasaunce."

Eastern Daily Press.

"The Meare and Club-house at the attractive bungalow seaside village of Thorpeness, near Aldeburgh, were opened yesterday by Lord Huntingfield in the presence of a large and fashionable gathering. This, the latest enterprise of Seaside Bungalows, Ltd., has undoubtedly added to the many natural charms of what is a unique watering-place on the East coast."

Norfolk News.

"Since the Kursaal was opened last year by Sir Wm. Bull, M.P., pretty wooden and tiled bungalows have sprung up on the sand dunes in close proximity to the sea. These charming Summer residences, with their striking red roofs, are dotted about in the most picturesque manner and Thorpeness promises to become, as it grows, one of the most delightful resorts on the lower part of the Suffolk coast."

Lowestoft Weekly Press.

"None of the old-time beauties of the place have been destroyed and with its splendid stretch of beach and undulating dunes, Thorpeness, with its added attractions of the Meare should find a large share of holiday patronage."

Suffolk Chronicle.

"On the lake have been placed a fine fleet of row boats, including skiffs, prams and dinghies, along with a squadron of Una-rigged centreboards especially constructed for this class of water." (*Illustration of Thorpeness Meare Boat-club on the lake.*)

Manchester Guardian.

"Illustration: "Rescuing a lake from an attack of weeds." Large photograph showing the operation of a Seine net, which was so successfully used at Thorpeness Meare to clear the weeds which in the early part of the season grew with such strength and rapidity as to threaten to render the lake useless for boating.

Leiston Observer.

"THE KURSAAL CONCERTS. Thorpeness is still crowded with visitors. Amongst others who have taken bungalows this September are SIR EDWARD and LADY EVERY, the HONBLE. MRS. H. A. LAWRENCE and MRS. DAVIES of Kelsale. SIR WILLIAM and LADY BULL also intended to spend their Summer at Thorpeness, with their family, but were unable to secure a bungalow. They have, however, been almost daily visitors with their children to the sands and Meare, where boating continues gaily. The privilege extended to non-members of taking tea between 4 and 6 p.m. on the loggia of the Club boat-house, has been largely taken advantage of by visitors from Aldeburgh. The third of the Concerts, which form such a delightful feature of the various diversions at the Kursaal, took place on Friday evening and was, if anything, more successful than the preceding ones ...... Altogether it was a very enjoyable evening, and MRS. GRANT deserves congratulation on the high character of her concert and the evident success with which it was attended."

The Aldeburgh Post.

"THE GARDEN VILLAGE BY THE SEA. Thorpeness is one of those places in which, during the past twelve months, change has followed change and improvement followed improvement, and this little bungalow township, with its magnificent stretch of sands extending along the whole foreshore, should prove a welcome addition to the attractions of the East coast. The developing Company—the Seaside Bungalows Ltd.—first brought Thorpeness into prominence by the erection of an up-to-date Kursaal, surrounded by attractive pleasure grounds, and since the opening of this building by SIR WILLIAM BULL, M.P., on May 6, 1912, the place has made remarkable progress, as is evidenced by the fact that no less than 30 new bungalows have been built or re-constructed."

Bury Free Press.

"As a safe seaside resort, for children especially, I do not know of a more delightful spot than this new 'bungalow town' of Thorpeness .... That Thorpeness will be a very popular place for children especially I have no doubt. It is a place formed by Nature for children."

Halesworth Times.

"The enterprising Directors of Seaside Bungalows Ltd. have spared no pains to make their latest completed project a success. The first President of the Club is SIR FREDERICK ADAIR, Bart."

CHAPTER IX.
EXCURSIONS IN THE VICINITY.

ALDRINGHAM.

About two miles from Thorpe, on the road to Leiston, lies the little village of Aldringham. Here by "The Parrot and Punchbowl" and the Post-office are four cross roads, leading respectively to Aldeburgh on the left, to Coldfair Green and Snape straight ahead, to Leiston on the right, the other road coming from Thorpeness itself. Behind the trees on the left as one enters the village is the Parish Church of St. Andrew, an ancient structure formerly appropriated to Leiston Abbey by Ranulph Glanville, the founder. Originally it possessed a tower, part of which is still shown standing in a water-colour sketch dated 1842. This sketch is now hanging in the vestry. The tower was afterwards razed to the ground, but the materials were not cleared away till 1843, when the whole of the West end was rebuilt, principally at the expense of Lord Huntingfield. In 1894, the late Miss Gannon inserted a stained East window in memory of her brother, and in the following year she presented the Church with carved oak furniture, consisting of reredos, Communion table and rails, pulpit, reading desk, and two carved stalls, etc. In 1896, the West window was filled with stained glass in Miss Gannon's memory. Joshua Chard, "the Suffolk hero," is buried in the churchyard. The Rev. T. W. Sedgwick is the present Vicar and Divine Services are held on Sundays in the Church as follows: Morning Prayer at 11, Evening Prayer at 3 p.m. Hamo de Masey, in the 12th of Edward II (1319) obtained a charter for a fair and market at Aldringham, which fair has long been obsolete, and the fair subsequently held on Coldfair Green ceased about 12 years ago. As already mentioned, the

Ogilvie Almshouses are near the Church, and on the way to Leiston is another row of very comfortable Homes for the Aged, also built by the late Margaret Ogilvie, and at present managed by the Ogilvie Charity Trustees.

ALDEBURGH

Lies about 1½ miles to the South of Thorpeness. Visitors from the bungalow town cross the Jubilee bridge and soon find themselves on a passably good road fringing the steep,

THE MOOT HALL.

shelving beach. The town takes its name from the river Alde, which runs near the South of it and affords a good quay at Slaughden.

The town is still governed by a Mayor and Corporation, having been newly incorporated in 1885.

Among the noteworthy features of the town, in addition to the Parish Church, are the Moot Hall, a very ancient and picturesque structure on the sea front, supposed to have been built in the 16th century, restored in 1854, and which now serves as a Court House and Police Station; the Lifeboat Station, where the records of the local braves tell of many a gallant deed upon the sea; the Public Hall and Library.

Aldeburgh Golf Club and its links are well-known to most players. Access is gained to it a short distance outside the town on the road to Saxmundham. There is a commodious Club-house, the whole course is kept in excellent order and a first-rate professional is employed.

Although the present means of communication are sadly defective it is possible to motor from Aldeburgh to Thorpeness along the sea front.

BLYTHBURGH

Lies to the North about 16 miles, via Leiston, Theberton, and Yoxford. Its chief glory is the Parish Church of the Holy Trinity, of which Suckling says: " Few ecclesiastical structures in this kingdom possess a juster claim to unqualified admiration than Blythburgh Church, a fabric splendid amidst decay and desolation."

The decadence of Blythburgh dates from the suppression of its Priory and the choking of the river, which spoiled it as a fishing port. Formerly it had quite a considerable fishery, and a gaol for the Beccles division. The Court House, where the Quarter Sessions were held, is now transformed into the

"White Hart" Inn, where the old carved ceilings and woodwork remain as relics of a once flourishing little town.

HOLY TRINITY CHURCH, BLYTHBURGH.

DUNWICH

Is but a shadow of its former self. Its Palace, its Churches, its Mint, its Docks, its "Mayer and three Baillies" are all things of the past. In 1754, when Gardner wrote his history, Divine Service was performed once a fortnight in All Saints' Church, which was then the only sacred edifice in use. This, however, was discontinued altogether about the period just mentioned, when the last great inroad of the sea was made on Dunwich. Only a few bare walls of the old Church now stand on the edge of the cliff, while close by are the ruins of the Franciscan Friary.

Mr. H. R. Tweed, in the "Westminster Cathedral Chronicle" of November, 1912, from which by the kindness of the Editor we are permitted to quote, thus describes the locality as it appears to-day: "As we approach across the purple moor, the ruins of All Saints' Church confront us, standing gaunt on Dunwich Cliff against the sunlit sky. On the same cliff, a few yards further inland, are the ruins of the Franciscan Friary, covering an area of some five acres, surrounded by its ancient wall. The main gateway still stands, and a few of the monastic buildings. This convent was founded by Richard Fitzjohn and Alice, his wife, to whose benefactions King Henry III made considerable additions.

Dunwich is some nine miles distant from Thorpeness, via Leiston, Theberton and Westleton.

RUINS OF FRANCISCAN FRIARY.

FRAMLINGHAM

Can be reached either by train from Leiston (change at Saxmundham and Wickham Market) or road, distance about 17 miles. The ancient Castle ruins and the modern Albert Memorial College are the glory of the town. A lady writer, Mrs. Berlyn, thus effectively described the place: "The artist who once finds himself here is not easily lured hence again, since not only the ruined castle, whose towers and walls are well-nigh shrouded with great masses of ivy, but the church, the park, and indeed the whole surrounding district is full of the most beautiful pictures. The country that lies from the low, Dutch-like shore of Aldeburgh, through Orford and Butley to Woodbridge in the one direction, and Framlingham in the other, is full of varied beauty."

LEISTON,

Three miles from Thorpeness, on the G.E.R., is the most convenient Station for the new seaside resort. A covered-in motor meets all trains by appointment. In 1778 Mr. Richard Garrett started ironworks for the manufacture of agricultural implements. Richard Garrett & Sons are now one of the largest manufacturers of steam tractors, agricultural implements, &c., in the kingdom. They send their tractors, &c., to Russia, Germany, Egypt, Persia, India, and indeed all over the globe. The prizes awarded them at various shows now form an extensive collection.

LEISTON ABBEY.

About a mile outside the town, on the road to Theberton, are the ruins of a fine old Abbey, formerly ruled by the Præmonstratensian White Canons. From an interesting article by Mr. H. R. B. Tweed, published in "The Westminster Cathedral Chronicle" of Nov., 1912, we take the following: "Leiston Abbey was founded in 1182 by Ranulph de Glanville, Justiciary of England, and was dedicated to the Blessed Virgin. He endowed it with the Manor of Leiston, and the churches of St. Margaret Leiston, St. Andrew Aldringham, of Middleton, and of Culpho, for the good estate of King Henry, his own soul's sake, and that of his wife Bertha, their ancestors and successors." The original Abbey was built nearer the sea, but in 1363 was rebuilt in its present position by its munificent benefactor and patron, Robert de Ufford, Earl of Suffolk.

ORFORD,

Some 12 miles distant by road, is well worth visiting. The church, with its ruined chancel dated at 700, and the Norman keep of the old Castle both bear testimony to brighter days when Orford was a comparatively large town and the centre of a considerable trade. It possessed a market as early as the reign of King Stephen; and in 1359 sent three ships and 62 men with the English invading fleet to Calais.

The massive strength of the Castle walls is astonishing; they are said to be 20-ft. wide at their foundation. No information is available either as to its builder or the date of its construction; but its Norman origin is inferred from the fact that it was coigned and in some places cased with Caen stone. In the days of Robert de Ufford the castle was evidently a formidable stronghold. There is still a room where visitors may picnic by permission, and the view from the top of the walls is splendid.

KEEP OF ORFORD CASTLE.

SIBTON,

Eleven miles distant from Thorpeness, is described in an old History of Suffolk as "a straggling village, on the river Minsmere, 2 miles West of Yoxford, 5 miles North by West of Saxmundham." It includes the hamlet of Sibton green. William de Casineto, or Cheney, founded a Cistercian Abbey at Sibton about the year 1150, and dedicated it to the Blessed Virgin. The Abbot and Convent themselves granted their property to Thomas, Duke of Norfolk, Anthony Rous, Esq., and Nicholas Hare, in 1536. Some ruins still exist, including part of the walls of the refectory and a portion of the chapel; and other remains of this once splendid edifice may be seen in the walls of the Abbey House.

SNAPE.

"Five miles to the West of Aldeburgh, across a breezy heath," says Mr. Tweed, "lies the site of Snape Priory founded in 1155 by William and Albreda Martel and Geoffrey, their son. It was constituted a cell to the Benedictine Convent of St. John of Colchester and endowed with the Manors of Snape and Aldeburgh; as an acknowledgment of submission the Priory paid half a mark of silver to St. John's Convent."

The river Alde, rising at Framlingham, widens into a tidal estuary at Snape, and flows straight for the sea until it reaches Aldeborough. There, unable to force the high shingle beach separating it from the sea, it heads Southwards and runs parallel with the sea for 12 miles before it finally blends its waters with the North Sea.

SOUTHWOLD.

Mr. H. R. B. Tweed says: "Southwold (Saxon: Sudwald— *i.e.* Southwood) possesses a fine perpendicular Church, built

ST. EDMUND'S CHURCH, SOUTHWOLD.

at the end of the 15th and beginning of the 16th centuries, on the site of a chapel which was a chapel of ease to Reydon

Church two miles away, and subject to the Priory of Thetford. Southwold Manor belonged to the Abbey of Bury S. Edmund's. The present Church is dedicated to St. Edmund, it is 144 feet long and 56 feet wide, with a western tower 100 feet high. It contains a beautiful Rood screen of carved wood, with painted portraits of the saints in the panels."

After the Reformation a blight fell on the place. In 1659 it was practically destroyed by fire, 238 houses, with the market place, town hall, granaries, warehouses, and shops having been consumed.

But, like a Phœnix, it has risen from its ashes again, and is now a popular and prosperous watering place.

YOXFORD,

Nine miles distant, via Leiston and Theberton, affords a delightful run through some of the prettiest country to what is often called "The Garden of Suffolk," on the banks of the small river Yox. It includes two manors, one of which formerly belonged to the monks of Thetford and the other to Sibton Abbey. S. Peter's Church, the parish fane, is in the Perpendicular style, with a tower containing six bells and surmounted by a leaded spire. It contains many mural monuments of the Blois family.

ADVERTISEMENTS.

Daimler

Open Testimony.

THE prevalence of Daimler Cars on the streets of London and in other centres of wealth and fashion is open testimony of their popularity. ✣ ✣ ✣ For good appearance and good service they are unrivalled. ✣ ✣ ✣ For real hard work the Daimler engine stands supreme, as is proved beyond doubt by the results of their use in the motor omnibuses of London and elsewhere. ✣ ✣ ✣ Watch the cars as they pass; it will not take an hour to convince you that the car you should buy is a Daimler.

Daimler Cars 1914
Four Speeds :: Electric Light :: Electric Starter

Twenty. Thirty. Special.
Four Cylinders : Four or Six Cylinders : H.M. The Queen's New Car

The Daimler Company, Ltd.
:: :: :: COVENTRY :: :: ::

LONDON SHOWROOMS :: 27, PALL MALL

Daimler Cars are held in readiness for immediate hire.

Telephone Regent 4160.

DEPOTS:

BIRMINGHAM Daimler House, Paradise Street	MANCHESTER 60, Deansgate
BRIGHTON - - St. John's Road, Hove	NEWCASTLE St. Mary's Place
BRISTOL - - - 61, Victoria Street	NOTTINGHAM 98, Derby Road
CARDIFF - - - - - Park Street	OXFORD - Osberton Road
LEEDS - - - - 82, Albion Street	TORQUAY - Torwood Street

Used by SEASIDE BUNGALOWS, Ltd., on the THORPENESS ESTATE.

Patent Excelsior Stone Cisterns and Cesspools

Also used by the Norfolk, Huntingdonshire, Berkshire, Oxford, Shropshire, Surrey, and numerous other County Councils for their Small Holdings. Largely used for Country Residences, Estate Cottages, Farm Buildings, &c. **Cheaper than galvanized iron, more sanitary, more durable.**

The only building material that increases in strength and hardens by age and exposure.

Awarded Gold Medal & Diploma, Crystal Palace (Small Holdings Exhibition), Oct., 1911.

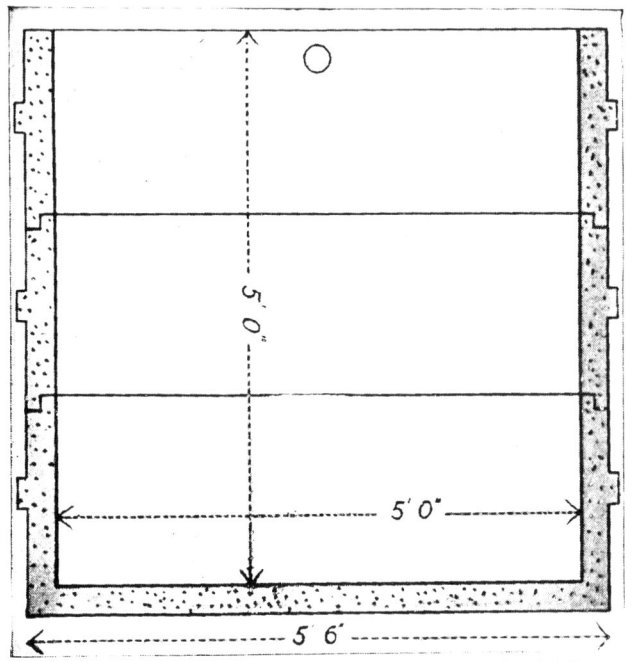

Capacity 650 Gallons.

Price: £8 : 0 : 0.

Cover Slab with Manhole and loose Lid with Lifting Ring, £1 extra.

Extra Rings, 45/- each.

Absolutely Watertight and of everlasting life.

CIRCULAR ON PLAN. 5 ft. diam.; 5 ft. high.

Can be fixed either Above or Below Ground.

EXCELSIOR STONE CISTERNS are made in Rings, heavily reinforced, and have rebated watertight joints as shown in illustration above. Each ring is fitted and numbered before being sent out and Lugs are cast on the outside of each ring, as shown, to aid slinging, minimizing labour in fixing them to the greatest possible extent.

SMALLER SIZES ALSO SUPPLIED.

The EXCELSIOR PATENT STONE Co.,
Finedon Sidings, NORTHAMPTONSHIRE.

EXCELSIOR STONE PAVING FLAGS

YARD PAVED WITH EXCELSIOR STONE FLAGS.

Plain Excelsior Stone Paving Flags for Yards, Paths, Terraces, etc.
2 ins. thick at 3/- per square yard at Works.
2½ ins. thick at 3/9 per square yard at Works.
Large Stocks always ready for immediate delivery.

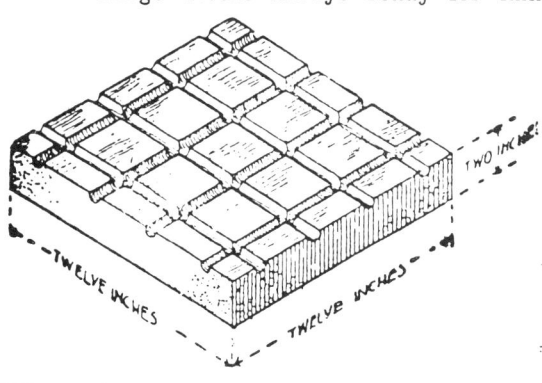

Grooved Stable Paving Slabs,
Price, 4/- per sq. yard.

Write for particulars of Excelsior Stone Cowstall and Stable Mangers, Reinforced Division Slabs Drinking Troughs and other Estate Goods.

Excelsior Patent Stone Co., Finedon Sidings, NORTHANTS.

EXCELSIOR STONE FLAGS

For Pavements, Paths, Yards, Motor Houses, etc.

Supplied to the principal Municipal, County, Urban and Rural Authorities, Railway Companies, etc.

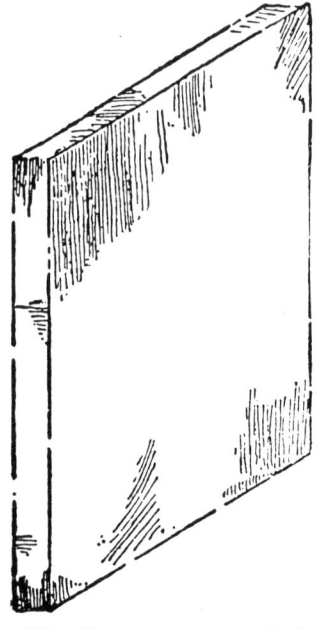

Excelsior Stone Paving Flags are supplied in the following sizes:—

3 ft. 0 in. by 2 ft. 0 in. by 2 in. thick
2 ft. 9 in. by 2 ft. 0 in. by 2 in. ,,
2 ft. 6 in. by 2 ft. 0 in. by 2 in. ,,
2 ft. 3 in. by 2 ft. 0 in. by 2 in. ,,
2 ft. 0 in. by 2 ft. 0 in. by 2 in. ,,
1 ft. 9 in. by 2 ft. 0 in. by 2 in. ,,
1 ft. 6 in. by 2 ft. 0 in. by 2 in. ,,

At 5d. per foot super, Carriage Paid at Leiston Station.

Same sizes, 2½ in. thick

At 6d. per foot super.

The flags are very similar in appearance to Portland Stone Flags at little more than half the cost, and are of practically everlasting wear.

DRAIN AND MANHOLE COVERS

3 ft. 0 in. by 3 ft. 0 in. by 3 in.   3 ft. 0 in. by 2 ft. 0 in. by 3 in.
2 ft. 6 in. by 2 ft. 6 in. by 3 in.   2 ft. 6 in. by 2 ft. 0 in. by 3 in.

At 8d. per foot super.

Other sizes to suit requirements made specially at the same price.

With Rings let in at **1/-** per cover extra.

COAL SHOOT COVERS

2 ft. by 2 ft. by 3 in., with 12 in. circular rebated hole in centre, at **3/6** each.

All prices include for delivery, carriage paid at Leiston Station in minimum 4 ton lots.

Excelsior Patent Stone Co., Finedon Sidings, NORTHANTS.

EXCELSIOR STONE WINDOW SILLS

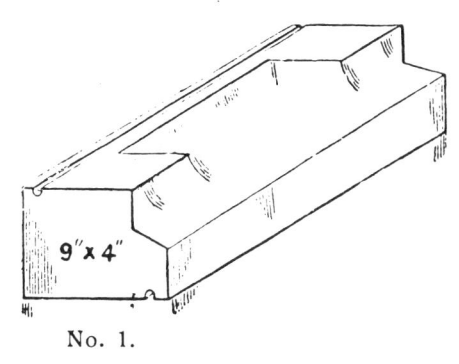

Weathered, Sunk, Stooled, Grooved, and Throated. For 4½-inch reveal, 3-inch stooling at each end.

For all usual openings.

9 in. by 3 in. (as illustration No. 1) 9d. per ft. lin.

9 in. by 4 in. (as illustration No. 1) 11d. per ft. lin.

11 in. by 6½ in. 1/9 ,,

9 in. by 6 in. 1/4 ,,

No. 1. 9"x 4"

THROATED WINDOW SILLS

(As illustration No. 2).

No. 2. 8½" 2½"

8 in. by 2½ in., in lengths to suit all usual openings ... 7d. per ft. lin.

9 in. by 3 in., in lengths to suit all usual openings ... 8d. per ft. lin.

12 in. by 3 in., in lengths to suit all usual openings ... 9d. per ft. lin.

Other Sizes and Designs specially quoted for.   Delivery at short notice.

DOOR STEPS.

9 in. by 3 in., square edge ... ... at 9d. per ft. lin.

11 in. by 3 in.,   ,, ... at 11d. ,,

ROUND NOSED STEPS ... at 1d. per ft. lin. extra.

9 in. by 6 in. ... ... at 1/4 per ft. lin.

12 in. by 6 in. ... ... at 1/9 ,,

14 in. by 6 in. ... ... at 2/1 ,,

18 in. by 3 in. ... ... at 1/4 ,,

MOULDED DOOR & WINDOW HEADS.

7 in. by 4½ in. ... ... at 9d. per ft. lin.

9 in. by 4½ in. ... ... at 11d. ,,

10 in. by 4½ in. ... ... at 1/- ,,

12 in. by 4½ in. ... ... at 1/3 ,,

4½ in. bearing each end.

Openings to correspond with all the above Sills.

Excelsior Patent Stone Co., Finedon Sidings, NORTHANTS.

Excelsior Patent Stone Pavors

These Pavors were awarded a Diploma at the Garden City Exhibition, held at Letchworth, near Hitchin, September, 1905.

EXCELSIOR PATENT STONE PAVORS in slabs 12 in. square and 9 in. square, 1 in. thick, are made in the usual natural stone colour and also in Black and Red.

The two colours laid alternately make a very neat and pleasing paving for hall entrance or verandah floors.

The colour of the Black Pavor is similar to that of a very dark Welsh Slate. The color of the Red Pavors is similar to that beautiful Stone **RED MANSFIELD.**

PRICES.

Black or Red Squares 12 in. by 12 in. by 1 in., at **3/-** per yard super. Halves at **3d.** each.

Portland Stone Cloured Squares 12 in. by 12 in. by 1 in. at **2/6** per yard super. Halves at **2d.** each.

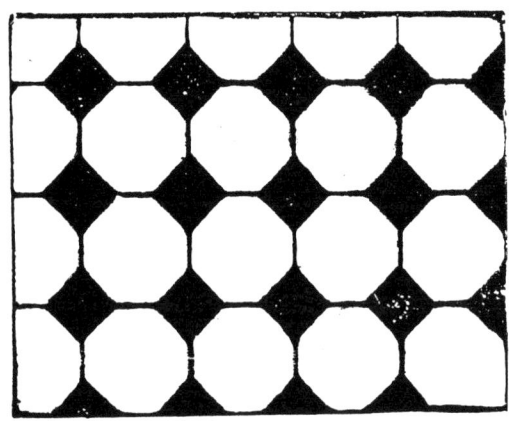

Portland Stone Coloured **Octagon Pavors** (as illustration), 12 in. by 12 in. by 1 in., at **2/9** per yard super, exclusive of Quarries for corners. 4 in. Special Black or Red Quarries for corners at **1d.** each. Diagonal Half and Quarter Quarries at **1d.** each.

2 in. thick Octagon Flags for Halls, Terraces, etc., 15 in. by 15 in. by 2 in., at **4/-** per yard super.

4 in. Quarries for same, as above, at **1d.** each.

All prices include for delivery, carriage paid at Leiston Station in minimum 4 ton lots.

Excelsior Patent Stone Co., Finedon Sidings, NORTHANTS.

RUBEROID

.. THE ..
ROOFING FOR

BUNGALOWS,
CLUB HOUSES, . . .
GARAGES,
AND ALL BUILDINGS .
REQUIRING A DURABLE,
ECONOMICAL ROOF OF
PLEASING APPEARANCE.

Made in three colours—Red, Grey, and Green, is suitable for flat pitched or curved roofs. Is proof against all weather and driving rains. Cool in Summer and warm in Winter. No painting or coating. Far longer life than iron or zinc. The first roofs laid over 20 years ago are still in perfect condition.

NO LEAKS.   **NO REPAIRS.**

Catalogue and Samples Free.

The RUBEROID COMPANY, Ltd.,
Roofing Manufacturers,
81-3, Knightrider Street, LONDON, E.C.

WM. C. READE

BUILDER & CONTRACTOR,

Principal Works carried out 1912-14.

30 Bungalows and various other Works at Thorpeness for Seaside Bungalows, Ltd.
F. FORBES GLENNIE, ESQ., Architect, *Selsey.*

House on Promenade at Aldeburgh for F. E. Barnes, J.P., Reigate.
E. PENFOLD, ESQ., A.R.I.B.A., Architect, *Reigate.*

New Council School at Pakefield, £5,177;
New Secondary School at Beccles, £6,577;
Re-modelling Junior Mixed School at Leiston for East Suffolk Education Committee.
J. WEBB, ESQ., Lic. R.I.B.A., *Ipswich.*

Two Houses at Waterloo Avenue, Leiston.
F. ANSTEAD BROWNE, ESQ., Lic. R.I.B.A., Architect.

Re-building Maltings at Beccles, £7,000, for Messrs. Jno. Crisp & Sons, Ltd.
F. W. SKIPPER, ESQ., Architect, *Norwich.*

Large House and Pair of Cottages at Aldringham for Mrs. A. M. Lay.
C. H. LAY, ESQ., A.R.I.B.A., Architect, *Aldringham.*

New Rifle Range at Sizewell for The War Office & Suffolk Territorial Association.
W. J. ROBERTS, ESQ., Architect, *Lowestoft.*

74, HIGH ST., ALDEBURGH.

Palgrave Brown & Son, Ltd.,

TIMBER IMPORTERS, . . .
ARBITRATORS & VALUERS,
"Yare" Sawing, Planing, & Moulding Mills,
**SOUTH TOWN, . . .
GREAT YARMOUTH.**

A large quantity of Timber, dry and well seasoned Deals and Floorings under cover, always in stock, also Lath, Pantile Splines, and every description of Scantling and Cut Stuff.

❧ ❧ ❧

MOULDINGS & SKIRTINGS in stock
And prepared to Order.

❧ ❧ ❧

MASTS, SPARS, POLES, OARS, QUANTS, BOAT-HOOK SHAFTS.

❧ ❧ ❧

SAWING AND PLANING
In all its Branches on the Cheapest Terms.

❧ ❧ ❧

☞ **HERRING BOXES and STAVES KEPT IN STOCK.**
Every description of Packing Cases cut to order.

N Telephone 136.
Telegrams: DAWBER,
Slater, Gt. Yarmouth.
Estab. 1789.

Head Office:
HULL.

TO ENSURE

Whether . .
covered with
SLATES, . .
FLAT TILES, or
ASBESTOS
ROOFING.

A SATISFACTORY
ROOF

YOU

Should place your Orders with a firm of
Practical Slaters and Tilers.

DAWBER, TOWNSLEY & Co., Ltd.

—OF—

YARMOUTH,

HULL,
GRIMSBY,
DARLINGTON,
STOCKTON-ON-TEES
BRIDLINGTON,
SCUNTHORPE and
KING'S LYNN.

Have during their existence of 125 years, gained such an experience in roof covering, to rightly merit the title of **SPECIALISTS**. The estimates and prices of D., T. & Co., Ltd., while comparing favourably with other quotations, will always be for best work only of its respective kind, and its soundness will be guaranteed.

SHIPPERS, IMPORTERS & MERCHANTS

of every Class of SLATES, TILES, CEMENT, LIME, and
BUILDING MATERIALS.

LOCAL OFFICES, STORES AND WHARF—
SOUTHTOWN, GREAT YARMOUTH.

DAWBER, TOWNSLEY & Co., Ltd.

GLASS, Plate, Sheet, and Ornamental.
EMBOSSED AND BRILLIANT CUT.
LEAD LIGHTS & MEMORIAL WINDOWS.
Lead, Sanitary Goods and Brasswork, Paints, Oils, Colours, Paperhangings,

NICHOLLS & CLARKE, Ltd.,
WHOLESALE BUILDERS' IRONMONGERS,
SHOREDITCH, LONDON.

The FERNDEN FENCING COMPANY,

Bell Vale, HASLEMERE, Surrey.

.. Manufacturers of the ..
FERNDEN CLEFT CHESTNUT PALE FENCING and GATES.

Complete illustrated Catalogue forwarded on application.

PUDLO
MAKES CEMENT WATER-PROOF
KERNER-GREENWOOD & Co.
102 S. ANNS, KING'S LYNN.

For Damp Walls, Flooded Cellars, Flat Roofs.

When Building your BUNGALOW insist on the builder including "PUDLO" in the Cement Work. Cement is porous. Pudlo makes Cement waterproof and does not injure Cement but adds to its strength.

Write for free Booklet.

THREE ESSENTIALS

FOR

Up-to-Date Villas or Bungalows

ARE

YOUNG & MARTEN'S "DELIGHT" COOKERS,

"HUE" Patent BARLESS STOVES

AND

"SOLACE" PORCELAIN BATHS.

Have the Best—you pay no more by doing so.

Apply for fully Illustrated Catalogue FREE.
Dept. "R."

YOUNG & MARTEN, Ltd., Stratford, LONDON. E.

SOLIGNUM WOOD PRESERVING STAIN.

For the Woodwork of . .

Seaside Bungalows, .

Boat and Club Houses,

And the many other buildings of a like nature to be found on the Sea Coast there is nothing that gives the same pleasing and artistic effect as Solignum.

*Sir George Alexander's Bungalow at Chorley Wood.
All Woodwork treated with Solignum.*

The cheapest Wooden Structure is beautified and its appearance transformed by the soft mellow tone which Solignum gives, and from being an eyesore it becomes a patch of colour in perfect harmony with its surroundings.

Solignum can be applied easily and quickly by anyone and its cost is far less than paint.

Write for pamphlet to the Sole Makers—

MAJOR & Co., Ltd., HULL.

SMYTH'S

104, High Street, LEISTON,

- - CONTRACT - -

FOR BUILDING - - -
DECORATING - - HOUSES
ALTERATIONS TO

And respectfully solicit enquiries. Entrusted by SEASIDE BUNGALOWS, Ltd, with the erection of The KURSAAL, The BOAT HOUSE, and various Bungalows at Thorpeness.

FARMILOE'S CEILINGITE,

ALSO

DISTEMPERS in Various Shades.

NINE ELMS PAINT.

Their Celebrated HARD GLOSS PRESERVATIVE PAINTS.

| TELEGRAMS: | - | - | SMYTH | - | - | LEISTON. |
| TELEPHONE: | - | - | 12 | - | - | LEISTON. |

BLINDS and CASEMENT CURTAINS Estimated for and satisfaction assured.

WALL PAPERS from 2d. per piece. Mattresses Re-made and Furniture Recovered.

On your way to THORPENESS : : :
: : from LEISTON STATION call at
SMYTH'S Furnishing Warehouse, 104, High St.,
. . **LEISTON,** . .
where you will find an extensive assortment of
FURNITURE, BEDSTEADS and BEDDING,
CARPETS, GLASS and CHINA, and every requisite
required in BUNGALOW FURNISHING. You can
also Hire PIANOS, MAIL-CARS and PERAMS.

TELEGRAMS:	-	-	SMYTH	-	-	LEISTON.
TELEPHONE:	-	-	12	-	-	LEISTON.

ASBESTOS SLABS

(H.P. BRAND).
FOR INTERIOR & EXTERIOR WORK.

FIRE, DAMP, and ROT proof.

Photograph of New Criminal Courts of Appeal, Strand, London.
Half-Timbered. Our Slabs form exterior panels; roofed with our Terra Cotta Tiles.

STANDARD SIZES.—4-ft. by 4-ft., 6-ft. by 3-ft., 8-ft. by 4-ft., and from 5/32" to ½-inch in thickness. These Slabs are manufactured expressly to fill the requirements of the London County Council.

"H.P." ASBESTOS TILES.

An ideal material for the Roofing of Bungalows, etc., cheap and effective. They conduct over 70% less Sun Heat than Slates, and are more durable. Supplied in three colours.—Grey, Blue, and Terra Cotta.

Apply for samples and full details to:—

MACHIN & KOENIG,
Hare Court, 62, Aldersgate Street, LONDON. E.C.

Also at Manchester, Glasgow, Birmingham, Nottingham, Leeds & Belfast.

TELEPHONE (2 LINES): 4818, LONDON WALL.
TELEGRAMS: "COMPOBOARD, LONDON."

HIGH CLASS PANEL WOODS

OAK,

ASH,

BIRCH,

and

MAHOGANY

PLYWOODS

for

DADOES and

CEILINGS.

We stock a large variety of Woods to suit all Classes of Work.

We also supply various boards for ceiling & partition work, viz.:—

COMPOBOARD (Original Swedish Patent).
CEIL BOARD.   CALNO BOARD.

Apply for samples and particulars to:—

MACHIN & KOENIG,
Hare Court, 62, Aldersgate Street, LONDON. E.C.

Also at Manchester, Glasgow, Birmingham, Nottingham, Leeds & Belfast.

TELEPHONE (2 LINES): **4818, LONDON WALL**
TELEGRAMS: "**COMPOBOARD, LONDON.**"

E. L. HUNT, Ltd., IPSWICH & CHELMSFORD.

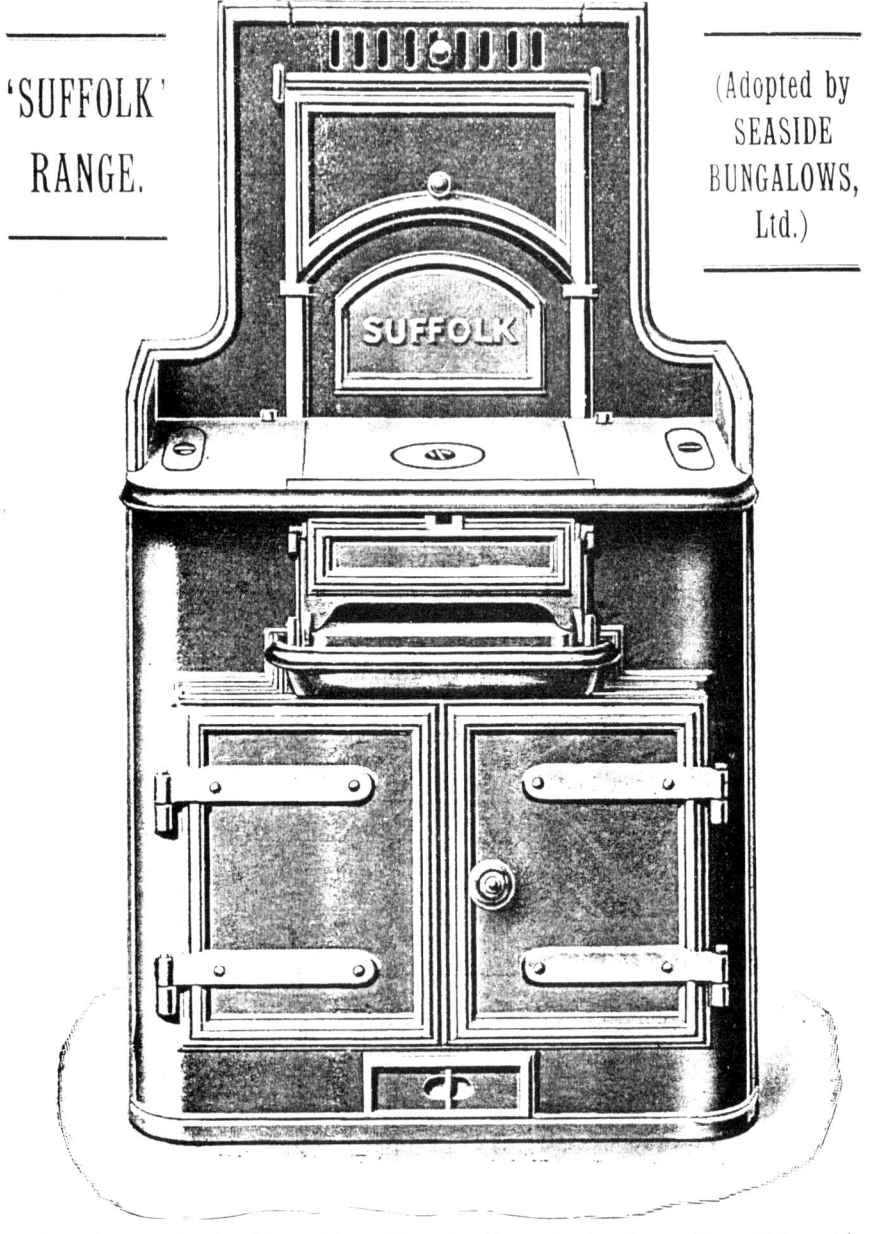

'SUFFOLK' RANGE.

(Adopted by SEASIDE BUNGALOWS, Ltd.)

Sizes kept in Stock: 24 in., 27 in., 30 in. by 40½ in. high. Large Oven 19 in. wide.

COMPLETE LIST ON APPLICATION.

E. L. HUNT, Ltd., IPSWICH & CHELMSFORD.

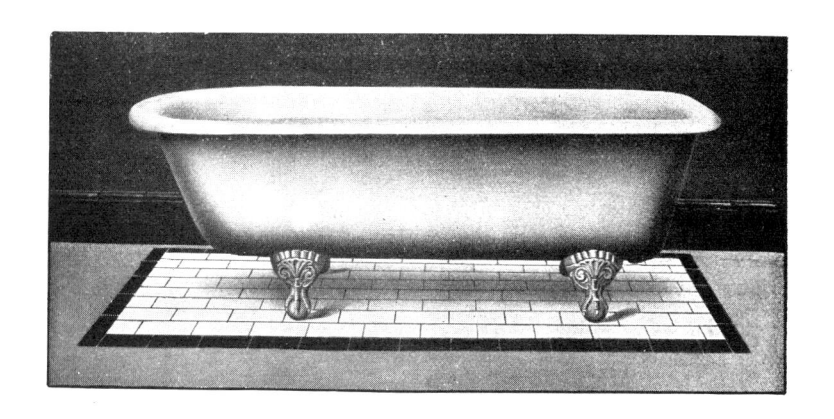

BATHS, LAVATORY BASINS, SINKS.
Large Stocks. Reasonable Prices.

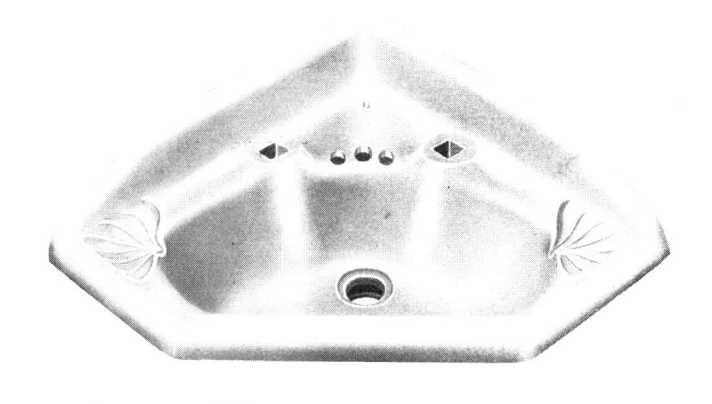

Large assortment of Locks, Latches, Window & Door Fasteners, and General Ironmongery

STOVES and **RANGES** of every description kept in Stock.

LARGE SHOWROOMS.

OLD ENGLISH GARDEN SEATS AND CHAIRS
The "TURVEY" Design.

SEAT.—Length, 4 ft.; width of seat, $16\frac{1}{2}$ ins.

Price in Deal, painted white or green	£1	5	0
,, English Oak, varnished	2	2	0
,, Teak, oiled	2	7	0

CHAIRS.

Price in Deal	£0	15	0
,, Oak	1	0	0
,, Teak	1	2	6

The above have been designed to meet a long felt want of a very light-weight, strong, comfortable garden seat and chairs.

Catalogue of Garden Seats sent upon application.

Messrs. John P. White & Sons, Ltd.,
The Pyghtle Works, Bedford.
London Showrooms: 123, NEW BOND STREET.

CARDON & CRESNO,

. . Manufacturers of the . .

"Cardon" Combined Chestnut Wood and Wire Fencing.

London Office: 61, 62, CHANCERY LANE, LONDON. W.C.

Works: PENSHURST STATION, KENT.

Prices from 6d. per yard.

PRICE LIST FREE ON APPLICATION.

Telephone: No. 1278, HOLBORN.

Telegrams: "CHESPALE, HOLB. LONDON."

The Best, Strongest, and most suitable Fencing for all purposes.

Unrivalled Exhibition Honours.

TWENTY-TWO GOLD, SILVER, and BRONZE MEDALS, DIPLOMAS OF HONOUR and Special Prizes, including the LEADING PRIZE FOR BEST SPECIMENS OF TAXIDERMY,

Only Gold Medal, 1881.

Were awarded at the Great International Fisheries Exhibition, London, 1883, to

T. E. GUNN, NATURALIST,

PRESERVER OF ANIMALS, BIRDS, REPTILES, FISH, &c.,

84 and 86, ST. GILES' STREET, NORWICH.

Also awarded upwards of **40** First Class Prizes (including **5** Gold Medals). Special Silver Cups and Silver Medals at National Exhibitions.

ESTABLISHED 1826.

WESTBROOKS'
Bakers & Confectioners,
High Street and Market Place, LEISTON.

ESTABLISHED 1860.

High-Class Bread a Speciality.

SCHOOL TEAS SUPPLIED.

☞ CAKES of every description.

Hovis, Wholemeal, ... and Milk Bread.

Daily Delivery at THORPENESS.

You can obtain . .

KODAK

And all Photographic Supplies,

BATHING CAPS,

TOILET PREPARATIONS,

and all Chemists' Sundries,

From S. L. GRAY, Chemist,
58, High St., LEISTON.

Try our Hazel Foam for Sunburn.

TABARD INN LIBRARY, Terms on Application.

DARK ROOM FOR AMATEURS.

Trees and Shrubs

Specially grown for Coast Planting.

Roses.

Awarded Two Gold Medals at the International Horticultural Exhibition, 1912. . . . .

Rose Garden in Woodbridge Nursery.

Landscape Gardening.

Water Gardens, Lawns, Paved Gardens, etc.

R. C. Notcutt,

The Nursery, Woodbridge.

James **PARRY & SONS,**

Maltsters

and Merchants,

HALESWORTH.

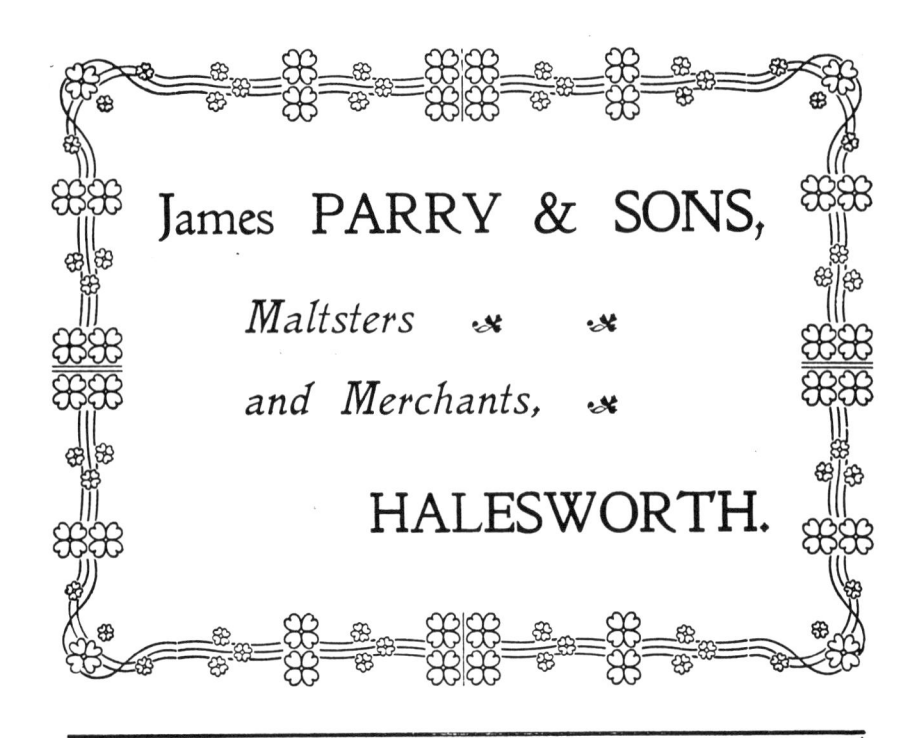

STANFORD & BROOM,

AUCTIONEERS AND

ESTATE AGENTS .

HALESWORTH,

SUFFOLK.

Incorporated
A.D. 1720.

ROYAL EXCHANGE, LONDON
HEAD OFFICE OF THE CORPORATION

Governor:
Sir Nevile Lubbock
K.C.M.G.

THE
ROYAL EXCHANGE ASSURANCE

undertakes nearly every class of Insurance, including Fire, Life, Sea, Accident, Burglary, Plate Glass, Motor Car, Employers' Liability, Fidelity Guarantees, Third Party, Live Stock.

Special terms are granted to Annuitants when health is impaired

The Corporation also undertakes the duties of

TRUSTEE & EXECUTOR

at minimum cost, and with complete protection to the beneficiaries.

Apply for full particulars to—
IPSWICH: St. Lawrence Chambers, 8, Butter Market,
C. W. DAVIES, Manager,
or to the Secretary, Royal Exchange, LONDON, E.C.

The "Leading Light"
Acetylene Gas Plant

500-light plant installed at Thorpeness.

PUBLIC INSTALLATIONS.

ACETYLENE GAS has now become an established form of lighting small Townships, Villages, Churches, Schools, Mansions, Factories, Workshops, etc., on account of its Illuminating Power, Ease of Installation, and Simplicity in Operation.

The Leading Light Syndicate, Ltd., have installed Acetylene at Thorpeness. The Installation consists of a Central Generating Station, and the Gas is conveyed through mains and service pipes to the Bungalows, etc. SLOT METERS have been provided, also GAS RINGS and OVENS. Thorpeness has the distinction of being the first Township in Great Britain to be equipped throughout with One Shilling Slot Meters and Cooking Apparatus.

PRIVATE INSTALLATIONS.

WE have during the last ten years lighted over 3,500 Country Mansions, Hotels, Houses, Churches, Chapels, and Works, and owing to the small cost of Installation, Acetylene undoubtedly is the cheapest and most economical light extant.

THE LEADING LIGHT SYNDICATE, Ltd.,
        PARROTT STREET, HULL.

Telephone No. 2871.   Telegrams: "Acetylene, Hull."

FOR WEEK ENDS.

THE ..

"Dolphin" Hotel,

THORPENESS.

(Under New Management).

Every Hotel Accommodation.

LUNCHEONS.   TEAS.   DINNERS.

GENERAL CATERING.

Agent for

ADNAMS' SOUTHWOLD
BOTTLED BEERS.

LIGHT BITTER ALE } 2/6 per doz.
EXTRA INVALID STOUT } Imperial Pints.

Quality.   Purity.   Condition.

WHITEWAY'S DEVONSHIRE }
GAYMER'S NORFOLK   ::   :: } CYDERS.

Bass.   Guinness.   Lager Beer.

—HIGH-CLASS MINERAL WATERS.—

TOURIST FORTNIGHTLY AND WEEK-END CHEAP TICKETS

FROM
London & Suburban Stations to Leiston
(For THORPENESS).

TOURIST. A.		FORTNIGHTLY. B.		FRIDAY or SATURDAY till TUESDAY. C.	
First.	Third.	First.	Third.	First.	Third.
27/9	16/9	25/0	13/0	16/0	10/0

A—Tourist tickets are issued by any train on any day and are available for return by any of the advertised trains on any day within six calendar months from the date of issue.

B—Fortnightly tickets are issued by any train on any day and are available for return by any of the advertised trains on any day within 15 days, including the days of issue and return.

C—Friday to Tuesday tickets are issued every Friday and Saturday by any train and are available for return by any of the advertised trains on the day of issue, or on any day (Sunday if train service permits) up to and including the Tuesday following.

LOCAL DAY EXCURSIONS FROM ALDEBURGH AND LEISTON
DURING THE SUMMER SEASON.

To IPSWICH, HARWICH, and FELIXSTOWE (Rail and Boat)— Every Thursday.

To FRAMLINGHAM— Every Thursday.

To SOUTHWOLD— Every Week-Day.

To YARMOUTH and LOWESTOFT— Daily.

ANGLO-AMERICAN OIL Co., Ltd.

Purveyors of Motor Spirit.

By Royal Warrant to H.M. the King.

PRATT'S PERFECTION SPIRIT

Pre-eminent in Power.

Perfectly Pure, being double distilled

Popular Everywhere because of its Reliability and Economy.

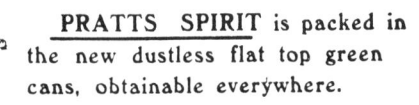

PRATTS SPIRIT is packed in the new dustless flat top green cans, obtainable everywhere.

ANGLO-AMERICAN OIL CO., Ltd.
QUEEN ANNE'S GATE,
WESTMINSTER, S.W.

Telephone:
No. 17, Leiston.

Telegrams:
"Carr Bros., Leiston."

When you come to THORPE you will require : : : :

❖ COAL ❖

ORDER from—

CARR BROS.,

Coal Factors : and Merchants,

Station Road,

LEISTON.

Local Agent:

BEN HARLING,

The Stores,

THORPE.

WHEN at THORPENESS

Always Shop at the . . .

THORPENESS STORES & POST OFFICE.

HIGH-CLASS PROVISIONS.

Daily Deliveries of Fresh Farm Butter, Eggs, Etc.

BATHING Costumes, Toys, General Drapery and Fancy Goods of all descriptions.

DECK CHAIRS, TENTS, BATH=CHAIRS, Etc., FOR HIRE.

Special View Post Cards of Thorpeness, 6d. per packet of 7 views, post free to any address.

W. SWALLOW,

Fruiterer, Greengrocer,

HIGH STREET,

LEISTON.

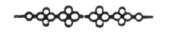

W. Swallow attends at Thorpe **EARLY EVERY MORNING** during the Season with a fine Selection of Choicest Seasonable FRUITS and VEGETABLES.

Bouquets, Wreaths, Crosses, etc., at Shortest Notice.

E. E. ALDRIDGE,

Family Butcher,

LICENSED TO DEAL IN GAME,

Salisbury House,

155-157, High St.,

ALDEBURGH.

Killer and Purveyor of the Primest and Best English Meat obtainable in the Town.

Salt Beef and Pickled Ox Tongues a Speciality. Prime Canterbury Lamb to Order.

Personal and Prompt Attention given to all Orders. 'Phone **14.**

BUTTS & SHARP, Ltd.,
"The Reliable Furnishers."

**FURNITURE DESIGNERS,
CABINET MAKERS & UPHOLSTERERS,
BEDSTEAD & CARPET FACTORS.**

BUNGALOW Furnishers.
House Furnishers.
Bank Furnishers.
Hotel Furnishers.
Office Furnishers.
Theatre Furnishers.
Government Contractors.

Furnishers to Seaside Bungalows, Ltd., Thorpeness.

SPECIALITÉ—THEATRE TIP-UP SEATING.
CATALOGUES & ESTIMATES FREE.

BUTTS & SHARP, Ltd.,
"The Reliable Furnishers,"
84-86, Canterbury Street, GILLINGHAM, Kent.
240, High Street, CHATHAM, Kent.

'PHONES { GILLINGHAM, 71.
         { CHATHAM, 603.

THORPENESS KURSAAL

BALCONIES :--

East, OVERLOOKING THE SEA AND SANDS;
West, OVERLOOKING THE TENNIS COURTS, CROQUET LAWN AND FLOWER GARDENS.

CONCERT HALL for Public & Private Entertainments, Dances, etc., on hire.

Spacious Lounge, Card Room, Circulating Library, Ladies' and Gentlemen's Cloak and Dressing Rooms, and all the conveniences of a well-appointed Club-house.

PORTABLE "DHOOLIE" BATHING CABINS.
DAINTY TEAS.
EXCELLENT CELLAR.

Lowest Annual Subscription of any Club of similar accommodation on the East Coast.

Note: A few more Annual Members---up to 200---will be admitted after election, without Entrance fee.

Apply—MR. GRAEME KEMP, *Secretary*,
THORPENESS, Leiston.

A. EVERSON,

Launch : and : Boat : Builder,

"Phœnix" Works,
WOODBRIDGE, Suffolk.

**For
LAUNCHES,
SKIFFS,
DINGHEYS,
and
PRAMS.**

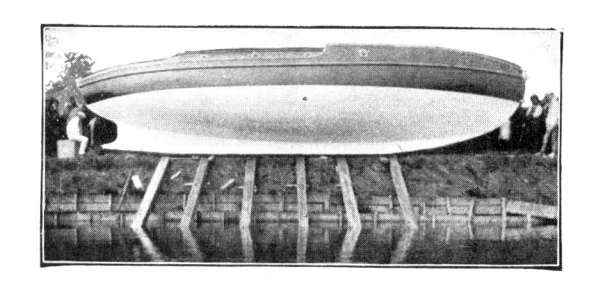

M.Y. "BUNYIP"—15 Tons.

Estimates Given.

Building, Repairs, and Installation.

Approx. weight
.. 140 lbs.

With Motor
.. 180 lbs.

☞ EVERSON'S PRAMETTE

From 10 feet. Draft—6 inches.

SAXMUNDHAM.

The "WHITE HART" HOTEL.

Visitors will find every comfort
and convenience at this

OLD ESTABLISHED FAMILY & COMMERCIAL HOTEL.

New Bathroom (H. & C.), and Lavatory.

☞ MOTOR CARS AND HORSES AND CARRIAGES ON HIRE

AT REASONABLE TERMS.

GARAGE.   PETROL.

Telegrams and Telephone: No. 9, SAXMUNDHAM.

Mr. & Mrs. JAS. FORSDIKE, Proprietors.

I. & J. ASHFORD, Limited,

Upholsterers and Decorators

Antique Dealers and Collectors,

SAXMUNDHAM and ALDEBURGH,

Hold one of the largest stocks in the Eastern Counties. Inspection invited.

HOUSEHOLD REMOVALS.

FURNITURE STORED in specially constructed Depository.

The "EN-TOUT-CAS" Hard Lawn Tennis Court.

(Patent No. 18734).

THE MOST POPULAR HARD COURT MADE!

(As laid at The Kursaal, Thorpeness).

We ARE making, HAVE MADE, and HAVE MORE orders on hand for Hard Courts, than ALL the other Hard Court Makers in this Country PUT TOGETHER.

700 MADE IN FOUR YEARS.

OVER 100 in course of construction or on order.

Recent Testimonials. . . .

Mr. A. F. WILDING, THE WORLD'S CHAMPION, ordered an "En-Tout-Cas" Court some time ago, has had six months' play on it and has now given us a repeat order for a further Court. He says that the "En-Tout-Cas" Court is the BEST.

Mr. R. B. POWELL, THE WELL-KNOWN CANADIAN PLAYER, writes:—17th October, 1913. "Having played on Hard Courts of every description in Europe, the United States, Canada, and South Africa, I have pleasure in stating my conviction that the "En-Tout-Cas" Hard Court is the best Hard Court at present in existence."

We have now 12 Expert Foremen on our Staff, and these men have been specially trained to make our Courts.

Before deciding upon your Hard Court write us for illustrated booklet, testimonials, etc., from noted players, authorities, and architects. Our clients will convince you of the success of the "En-Tout-Cas" Courts.

The "EN-TOUT-CAS" Co., Ltd., 30, Great St. Helens, E.C.

Nat. Tel.: 5 Syston.   Works: Syston, near Leicester.   Telegrams: Tennis Co., Syston.

Telegrams: "Dennington, Halesworth."   Telephone: No. **7.**

DENNINGTON & Co. (1910) Ltd.,
Sack, Rick Cloth, & Tent Manufacturers, & Contractors,
HALESWORTH.

TENTS and MARQUEES Let on Hire.
All sizes.   Men sent to fix and remove same.   Prices on application.

WHEN visiting Thorpeness and District, and requiring any ARTICLES for PRESENTS, etc., visit . . .

H. E. JOLLY,
Watchmaker, Jeweller, and Optician,

High Street, SAXMUNDHAM,

Who keeps a nice Selected Stock of SUITABLE GOODS.

REPAIRS in all Branches of the Trade.

Established 1769.

WELL WORTH A VISIT.

Carters Model Establishment
at RAYNES PARK.

All who are interested in Gardening

ARE INVITED TO INSPECT

our Model Warehouse & Machinery and see how

CARTERS TESTED SEEDS

are cleaned and the growth tested before being despatched to customers all over the world.

COME AGAIN

in the Summer and look over the five miles of Pea Trials and other interesting and instructive sights in our EXPERIMENTAL GROUNDS. If you cannot spare time to make a personal call, then write for

Illustrated Catalogue of Garden Seeds.   Post Free.

Carters TESTED SEEDS

SEEDSMEN TO
H.M. THE KING.

RAYNES PARK, LONDON, S.W.

POTTER & WIGHTMAN,

MOTOR and CYCLE ENGINEERS
-:-　 -:-　and AGENTS,　-:-　-:-
High Street, LEISTON.

OPEN AND CLOSED CARS FOR HIRE.
SPECIAL QUOTATIONS FOR LARGE PARTIES.
Meet Trains by Appointment.

Large Stock of Cycles by best makers on the Premises for Sale and Hire on Reasonable Terms. ❧ Motor ❧ Tyres, etc., at Store Prices. ❧

OVER 20 YEARS PRACTICAL EXPERIENCE.

CUTHBERT, ❧

Outfitter, LEISTON,

FOR ❧ ❧ ❧

FLANNEL TROUSERS,

SPORTS JACKETS, ❧

AND

COOL COMFORTABLE

SHIRTS. ❧　❧　❧

LONDON GOODS AT LESS THAN LONDON PRICES.

ALLIANCE
ASSURANCE COMPANY, LIMITED.
(Established in 1824)

Head Office - - BARTHOLOMEW LANE, LONDON.

Assets exceed £23,500,000.

Chairman—The Right Honble. LORD ROTHSCHILD, G.C.V.O.
General Manager—ROBERT LEWIS.

SUFFOLK OFFICES.

IPSWICH.
OFFICES: QUEEN STREET.

BOARD.
Right Hon. LORD RENDLESHAM, Chairman.
FRANCIS LAWRENCE BLAND, Esq.
HERBERT ST. G. COBBOLD, Esq.
CHARLES CUTHBERT ELEY, Esq.
CHARLES JAMES GRIMWADE, Esq.
HENRY MASON JACKAMAN, Esq.
GEORGE JARVIS NOTCUTT, Esq.
EDWARD PACKARD, Esq.
CHARLES RICHARDS STEWARD, Esq.
RICHARD EDWARDS, *Secretary*.

BURY ST. EDMUND'S.
OFFICES: ABBEYGATE STREET.

BOARD.
J. KIRBY RODWELL, Esq., Chairman.
The Most Hon. The MARQUESS OF BRISTOL.
A. BECKFORD BEVAN, Esq.
SIR E. WALTER GREENE, Bart.
JOHN W. GREENE, Esq.
JAMES J. SPARKE, Esq.
ROWLAND H. WILSON, Esq.
ALAN ROSS CHRISTOPHERSON, *Secretary*.

The operations of the Company extend to the following, among other Branches of Insurance:—

FIRE.   LIFE & ANNUITIES.   MARINE.
CONSEQUENTIAL LOSS FOLLOWING FIRE.
WORKMEN'S COMPENSATION.
PERSONAL ACCIDENT AND DISEASE.
THIRD PARTY AND DRIVERS' RISKS.
PLATE GLASS AND HAIL-STORM.
BURGLARY AND THEFT.
FIDELITY GUARANTEE.

The Company also grants
CAPITAL REDEMPTION POLICIES.

The Directors invite proposals for Loans on, and for the Purchase of Reversions and Life Interests.

Prospectuses and Proposal Forms may be had on application to any of the Company's Offices or Agents.

VISITORS to THORPENESS and District can obtain

Medicines dispensed accurately and quickly.
Drugs and Chemicals of the Purest Quality.
Patent Medicines, Toilet Articles, and Sundries at lowest London Store Prices.

Photographic Requisites of all kinds.
Developing, Printing, and Enlarging at short notice.
Depot for Kodak Goods.

CHARLES HARDY, M.P.S.,
7, HIGH STREET, LEISTON.

Telephone No. 25, Leiston.

Telephone No. 2.

William Catling,

PURVEYOR,

HIGH STREET, LEISTON.

Families waited on Daily for Orders at Thorpeness.

FRESH PORK SAUSAGES DAILY.

Home-Bred and Scotch Beef.

Prime Suffolk and Southdown Mutton.

Dairy Fed Pork.

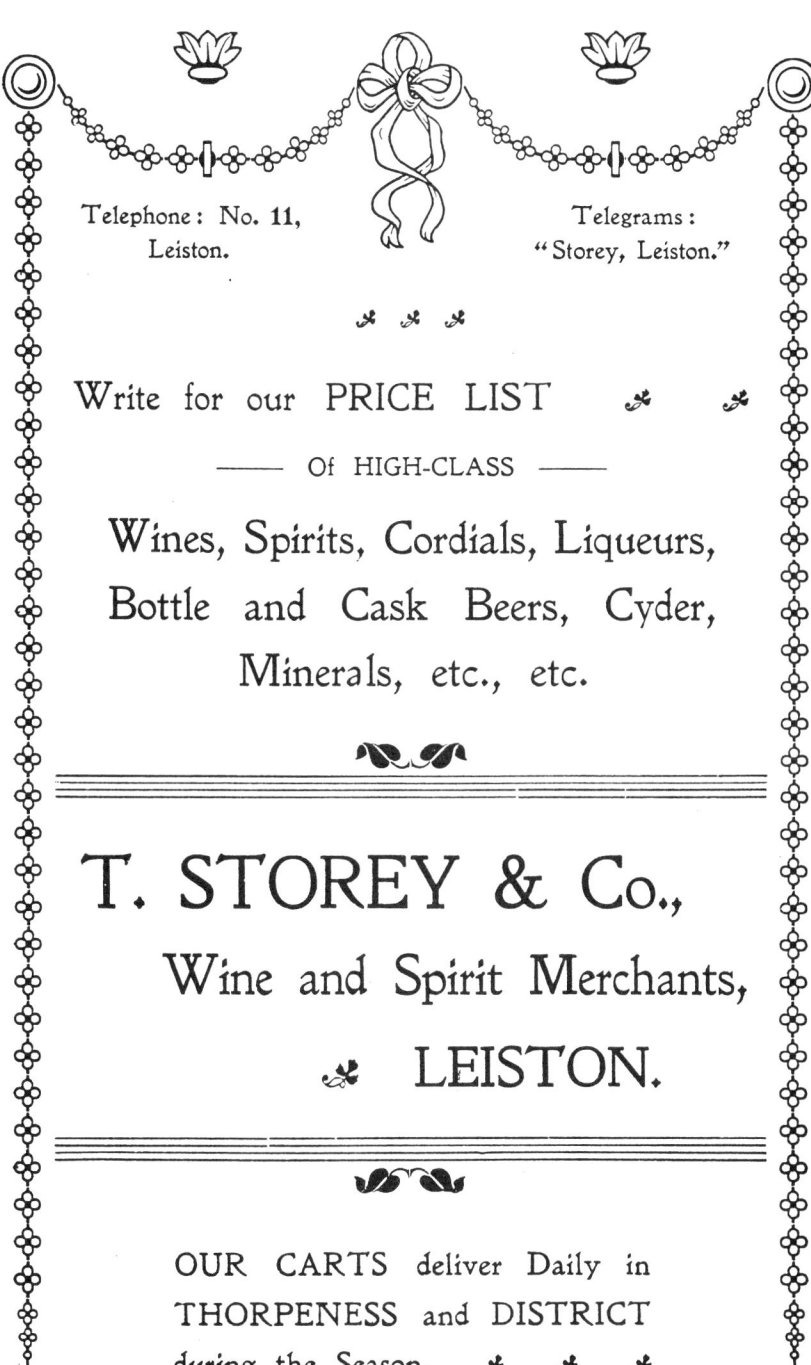

Telephone: No. **11**, Leiston.

Telegrams: "Storey, Leiston."

Write for our PRICE LIST

—— Of HIGH-CLASS ——

Wines, Spirits, Cordials, Liqueurs, Bottle and Cask Beers, Cyder, Minerals, etc., etc.

T. STOREY & Co.,

Wine and Spirit Merchants,

LEISTON.

OUR CARTS deliver Daily in THORPENESS and DISTRICT during the Season.

GREY & MARTEN, Ltd.,
Manufacturers and Merchants, = =
SOUTHWARK BRIDGE, LONDON, S.E.

Specialities:—
PAINTS, VARNISHES, Etc.

STOVES, RANGES, BATHS, ETC.

❧ Specify our Goods through your Builder. ❧

TELEPHONE 45.

G. SMITH,
Baker, Confectioner and Caterer,
The Hygienic Steam Machine Bakery,
190 & 181, High St., ALDEBURGH-on-Sea.

All kinds of FLOUR, BREAD, CAKES, and PASTRY of the very best quality.

☞ **TEAS, REFRESHMENTS, and ICES.**

Bread Delivered Daily to all parts of the Town and Country.
Dr. Allinson's Whole-meal Bread.
HOVIS, Vienna and Milk Bread. Fancy Rolls.

OUR GOODS ARE OUR BEST RECOMMENDATION.

FAMILIES SUPPLIED DAILY AT THORPENESS.

THE WHISKY THAT NEVER VARIES

OLD GAOL WHISKY
(SCOTCH OR IRISH)

MATURED BY AGE
ABSOLUTELY SOUND
ALWAYS THE SAME

This grand old Whisky is famed for its creamy mellow flavour, the result of expert blending, and careful maturing. It does not vary, and you can be quite certain that one bottle will be as good as the last, because every drop is guaranteed at least 10 years old.

27/- Per Gallon.

4/8 Per Bottle.

Sold by
W. S. COWELL, Ltd.,
MARKET LANE, IPSWICH.

WARD'S GARAGE,
High Street, ALDEBURGH-ON-SEA.

*Motors and Bicycles Stored and for Hire. :—:
:—: Repairs, Accessories, Tyres, Oils stocked.*

G. E. R. CARTAGE AGENTS.

'BUSES and CABS to and from Station.
WAGGONETTES to Golf Ground.
CARRIAGES of all descriptions.

Orders to East Suffolk Hotel promptly attended to.
Telephone: No. 9.

GEO. E. GUNTHORPE,
Wholesale and Retail
GROCER AND PROVISION MERCHANT,
High Street, LEISTON.

Tea and Coffee Specialist.

FINEST BACON, BUTTER, AND CHEESE.

Customers waited on Daily.

PROMPT ATTENTION.
EXPRESS DELIVERY.

Thorpeness Boat Club.

Subscription: For one day, 1/-; week-end, 2/-; month, 5/-; or year, 10/-
Tickets including all members of a single Family, 12/6.

TEAS & OTHER REFRESHMENTS

served on the Loggia overlooking the landing stage and lake.

Non-members admitted to the Loggia for the purpose of Teas and Refreshments between the hours of 4 and 6 p.m.

Dressing rooms and lavatory accommodation for Ladies and Gentlemen. : : :

BOATING ON THE LAKE.

Una-rigged centre-boards, skiffs, dingheys, canoes, Thames punts for hire by hour, day or year.

"THE HOME OF PETER PAN."

The Blue Lagoon.   The Children's Paradise.
The Magic Pavilion.   Peggotty's House.
Roaring Camp.   The Brigands' Haunt.
The Pirates' Lair.   The Smugglers' Cave,
on Separate Islands, etc., for hire from 2/- the afternoon.

Tripods, kettles, fuel, and all necessaries for tea picnics supplied. : : :

For announcement of Venetian Fêtes, Regattas, Concerts, etc., see advertisements in Local Papers.

H. GRAEME KEMP,
Secretary, Boat Club,
THORPENESS

'The Aldeburgh Post'

Leiston, Saxmundham and
Thorpeness News.   =   =

The best and most influential ADVERTISING MEDIUM *in the Thorpeness District.*

⚜ ⚜ ⚜

THORPENESS VISITORS' LIST SUPPLIED
Regularly throughout the Season.

⚜ ⚜ ⚜

The "*Aldeburgh Post*" is the recognised Medium for all advertisements and news relating to Thorpeness and the District. Its circulation embraces the surrounding towns of Aldeburgh, Leiston, and Saxmundham. Its Postal circulation shows a steady and continuous increase, a fact which renders its advertisement columns of special value to clients desiring to let houses or apartments for the Summer Season.

On sale at numerous Agents throughout the district, or will be sent post free, on prepayment of 2s. 2d. for the half-year, on application to the HEAD OFFICE, THE NUTSHELL, LEE ROAD, ALDEBURGH.

"SHELL"   "PRATT'S"
MOTOR SPIRIT.

Greases and Oils.

BEST ENGLISH METHYLATED SPIRITS.

W. D. TITLOW & SON,

General and - - -
Furnishing Ironmongers,

High Street, LEISTON.

CRICKET & TENNIS REQUISITES.

SLAZENGER'S BALLS Stocked.

Agents for W. & A. GILBEY'S WINES and SPIRITS.

Thorpeness Vitesse Ltd.

A covered Motor Brake, to hold 11 persons meets any G.E.R. train at Leiston by appointment.

LUGGAGE DELIVERED AT PASSENGERS' RESIDENCES.

SPECIAL EXCURSIONS arranged throughout the Season to—ORFORD CASTLE, BLYTHBURGH CHURCH, LEISTON & DUNWICH ABBEYS, SOUTHWOLD, Etc., Etc.

Telephone: No. 22, LEISTON.   Telegrams: "VITESSE, THORPENESS."

For full information apply to—
Mr. GRAEME KEMP, Secretary,
Vitesse Ltd., THORPENESS, LEISTON.

HAZELL'S

Complete Shop & Office Fitters,

25, FORE STREET, IPSWICH,

UP-TO-DATE ELECTRIC WORKS.

Shop Fronts and Show-cases, Designs and Estimates submitted.

Personal and Prompt Attention to all Orders, large or small.

DISTANCE NO OBJECT.   Telephone: **36.**

GEO. DURRANT,

Ladies' and Gentlemen's Tailor,

4, Sizewell Road, LEISTON, and
Thoro'fare, WOODBRIDGE, - -

Has a large and well selected Stock for the coming season, suitable for

**LADIES' COSTUMES,
SPORTING SUITS,
BUSINESS SUITS,
MOTOR LIVERIES, Etc.**

All Goods made under my own supervision by experienced workmen.

LONDON STYLES AT COUNTRY PRICES.

IF YOU WANT

MINERAL WATERS

in bottles or syphons, you should be sure to ask for

TALBOT'S

The firm has been established over 70 years and anything bearing their name is thoroughly reliable.

BREWED GINGER BEER

in bottles or in convenient 1 or 2 gall. jars with tap.

LOCAL BRANCH: SAXMUNDHAM.

Head Office: TALBOT & Co., Ltd., 1, Crown Street, IPSWICH.

CERTIFICATE OF PURITY.—The National Union of Mineral Water Manufacturers certify that MESSRS. TALBOT & Co., LTD., have complied with their regulations, in respect of the Sanitary and Hygienic Conditions under which their waters are produced, and their products after examination by the Official Analyst are declared **ENTIRELY FREE FROM CONTAMINATION,** and to be pure and wholesome beverages. LONDON, JAN., 1914.

R. H. WARD,
Building Contractor
. and Well Sinker .

Orchard Road, LEISTON.

—·· ··—

All branches of Jobbing Work executed promptly and by expert Workmen.

—·· ··—

ESTIMATES FREE.

J. CUTTS & SON,
Undertakers, Builders, Contractors,

Cross Street, LEISTON.

Contractors to H.M. War Office, Board of Trade, and Admiralty.

—·· ··—

CUTTS' IMPROVED STEPS.

—·· ··—

ESTIMATES GIVEN for all kinds of Work.

Established 30 Years.